THE CONSTANT WIFE

A Play in Three Acts

by

W. SOMERSET MAUGHAM

SAMUEL  FRENCH

LONDON

NEW YORK TORONTO SYDNEY HOLLYWOOD

THE CONSTANT WIFE

Produced on 6th April, 1927, at the Strand Theatre, London, and revived on May 19th, 1937, at the Globe Theatre, London, with the following cast of characters :

(in the order of their appearance)

MRS. CULVER	*Helen Haye*
BENTLEY	*Victor Boggetti*
MARTHA CULVER	*Everley Gregg*
BARBARA FAWCETT	*Dorothy Lane*
CONSTANCE MIDDLETON	*Ruth Chatterton*
MARIE-LOUISE DURHAM	*Eileen Peel*
JOHN MIDDLETON, F.R.C.S. . . .	*Cecil Parker*
BERNARD KERSAL	*Cyril Raymond*
MORTIMER DURHAM	*Walter Piers*

SYNOPSIS OF SCENES

The action of the play takes place in John's house in Harley Street.

THE CONSTANT WIFE*

ACT I

SCENE: CONSTANCE MIDDLETON'S *drawing room. A summer
afternoon. It is a room furnished with singularly good taste.*
CONSTANCE *has a gift for decoration and has made this room of
hers both beautiful and comfortable. There are doors up* C., *leading
to the hall. Another door up* R. *leads to a morning room or a
library. The windows are* L. *and the fireplace* R. *At* R.C. *there
is a sofa. Up* L.C. *is a small grand piano, with a long music stool
below it.* (NOTE:—*If a piano is not available, another small settee
may be placed in the position of the piano stool, and above it
a round table on which may be set a bowl of flowers, one ot two
framed photographs or any other desired dressings.) There is
a writing desk at the window, a low table down* L., *and a small
easy chair below and* R. *of it. Another easy chair is set down* R.,
below the fireplace. (See the GROUND PLAN *at the end of the play.)*

When the CURTAIN *rises,* MRS. CULVER *is discovered seated on the
sofa, at the* L. *end, reading an illustrated periodical. She is an
elderly lady with a pleasant face and is dressed in walking costume.
After a few moments, the doors up* C. *open and* BENTLEY, *the
butler, enters. He is followed by* MARTHA CULVER, *who is* MRS.
CULVER'S *daughter and a fine young woman.*

BENTLEY. Miss Culver.

(He exits.)

MARTHA (*moving down a little and seeing* MRS. CULVER). Mother !
MRS. CULVER (*very calmly*). Yes, darling. (*She does not look up
from the page she is studying.*)
MARTHA (*moving to the* L. *end of the sofa*). You're the last person
I expected to find here. You never told me *you* were coming to see
Constance.
MRS. CULVER (*good-humouredly*). I didn't intend to till I saw in
your beady eye that *you* meant to. I thought I'd just as soon be
here first. (*She puts down the periodical.*)
MARTHA. Bentley says she's out.
MRS. CULVER. Yes. Are you going to wait ?
MARTHA (*crossing down to the fireplace*). Certainly.
MRS. CULVER. Then I will too.
MARTHA. That'll be *very* nice.
MRS. CULVER. Your words are cordial, but your tone is slightly
frigid, my dear.
MARTHA (*turning*). I don't know what you mean by that, mother.

---

*N.B. Paragraph 3 on page 2 of this Acting Edition regarding photo-
copying and video-recording should be carefully read.

5

MRS. CULVER. My dear, we've known one another a great many years, haven't we ? More than we always find it convenient to mention.

MARTHA. Not at all. I'm thirty-two. I'm not in the least ashamed of my age. Constance is thirty-six.

MRS. CULVER. And yet we still think it worth while to be a trifle disingenuous with one another. Our sex takes a natural pleasure in dissimulation.

MARTHA. I don't think anyone can accuse me of not being frank.

MRS. CULVER. Frankness, of course, is the pose of the moment. It is often a very effective screen for one's thoughts.

MARTHA (*moving in, to* R. *of the sofa*). I think you're being faintly disagreeable to me, mother.

MRS. CULVER. I, on the other hand, think you're inclined to be decidedly foolish.

MARTHA. Because I want to tell Constance something she ought to know ?

MRS. CULVER. Ah, I *was* right then. And it's to tell her that you've broken an engagement and left three wretched people to play cut-throat.

MARTHA. It is.

MRS. CULVER. And may I ask why you think Constance ought to know ?

MARTHA. Why ? *Why* ? (*Moving down* R. *to the easy chair*.) That's one of those questions that really don't need answering.

MRS. CULVER. I've always noticed that the questions that really don't need answering are the most difficult to answer.

MARTHA. It isn't at all difficult to answer. She ought to know the truth *because it's the truth*. (*She sits in the easy chair down* R.)

MRS. CULVER. Of course truth is an excellent thing, but before one tells it one should be quite sure that one does so for the advantage of the person who hears it rather than for one's own self-satisfaction.

MARTHA. Mother, Constance is a very unhappy person.

MRS. CULVER. Nonsense. She eats well, sleeps well, dresses well *and* she's losing weight. No woman can be unhappy in those circumstances.

MARTHA. Of course, if you won't understand it's no use my trying to make you. You're a darling, but you're the most unnatural mother. Your attitude simply amazes me.

(*The door opens and* BENTLEY *ushers in* MRS. FAWCETT. MRS. FAWCETT *is a trim, businesslike woman of forty*. MARTHA *rises*.)

BENTLEY. Mrs. Fawcett.

(*He exits*.)

MRS. CULVER. Oh, Barbara, how very nice to see you.

BARBARA (*crossing down and kissing her*). Bentley told me you were here and Constance was out. What are you doing ?

MRS. CULVER. Bickering.

BARBARA (*crossing below the sofa*). What about ? (*She sits* R. *of* MRS. CULVER.)

MRS. CULVER. Constance.

MARTHA (R. *of the sofa*). I'm glad you've come, Barbara . . . Did you know that John was having an affair with Marie-Louise ?

BARBARA. I hate giving a straight answer to a straight question.

MARTHA. I suppose *everyone* knows but us. How long have you known ? They say it's been going on for months. I can't think how it is we've only just heard it.

MRS. CULVER (*ironically*). It speaks very well for human nature that with the masses of dear friends we have it's only today that one of them broke the news to us.

BARBARA. Perhaps the dear friend only heard it this morning.

MARTHA. At first I refused to believe it.

MRS. CULVER. Only quite, quite at first, darling. You surrendered to the evidence with an outraged alacrity that took my breath away.

MARTHA. Of course I put two and two together. After the first shock I understood everything. I'm only astonished that it never occurred to me before.

BARBARA. Are you very much upset, Mrs. Culver ?

MRS. CULVER. Not a bit. I was brought up by a very strict mother to believe that men were naturally wicked. I am seldom surprised at what they do and never upset.

MARTHA. Mother has been simply maddening. She treats it as though it didn't matter a row of pins.

MRS. CULVER. Constance and John have been married for fifteen years. John is a very agreeable man. I've sometimes wondered whether he was any more faithful to his wife than most husbands, but as it was really no concern of mine I didn't let my mind dwell on it.

MARTHA. *Is* Constance your daughter, or is she *not* your daughter ?

MRS. CULVER. You certainly have a passion for straight questions, my dear. The answer is yes.

MARTHA. And are you prepared to sit there quietly and let her husband grossly deceive her with her most intimate friend ?

MRS. CULVER. So long as she doesn't know I can't see that she's any the worse. Marie-Louise is a nice little thing, silly of course, but that's what men like, and if John is going to deceive Constance, it's much better that it should be with someone we all know.

MARTHA (*to* BARBARA). Did you ever hear a respectable woman— and mother is respectable . . .

MRS. CULVER (*interrupting*). Oh, quite.

MARTHA. . . . talk like that ? (*She turns down to the fireplace.*)

BARBARA. You think that something ought to be done about it ?

MARTHA (*turning to face them*). I am determined that something shall be done about it.

MRS. CULVER. Well, my dear, I'm determined that there's at least one thing you shan't do, and that is to tell Constance.

BARBARA (*to* MARTHA; *a trifle startled*). Is that what you want to do ?

MARTHA. Somebody ought to tell her. If mother won't, I must.

BARBARA. I'm extremely fond of Constance. Of course, I've known what was going on for a long time, and I've been dreadfully worried.

MARTHA (*moving a pace towards the sofa*). John has put her into an odious position. No man has the right to humiliate his wife as he has humiliated Constance. He's made her perfectly ridiculous.

MRS. CULVER. If women were ridiculous because their husbands are unfaithful to them, there would surely be a great deal more merriment in the world than there is.

BARBARA (*delighted to have a good gossip*). You know they were lunching together today ?

MARTHA. We hadn't heard that. But they were dining together the night before last.

MRS. CULVER (*brightly*). We know what they had to eat for dinner. Do you know what they had to eat for lunch ?

MARTHA. Mother ! (*She moves down again to the fireplace.*)

MRS. CULVER. Well, I thought she seemed rather uppish about the lunch.

MARTHA. You have no sense of decency, mother.

MRS. CULVER. Oh, my dear, don't talk to me about decency. Decency died with dear Queen Victoria.

(MARTHA *sits, down* R.)

BARBARA (*to* MRS. CULVER). But you can't approve of John having an open and flagrant intrigue with Constance's greatest friend.

MRS. CULVER. It may be that with advancing years my arteries have hardened. I am unable to attach any great importance to the philanderings of men. I think it's their nature. John is a very hard-working surgeon. If he likes to lunch and dine with a pretty woman now and then, I don't think he's much to blame. It must be very tiresome to have three meals a day with the same woman for seven days a week. I'm a little bored myself at seeing Martha opposite me at the dinner-table. And men can't stand boredom as well as women.

MARTHA. I'm sure I'm very much obliged to you, mother.

BARBARA (*significantly*). But they're not only lunching and dining together.

(MARTHA *sits erect and looks at* BARBARA.)

MRS. CULVER. You fear the worst, my dear ?

BARBARA (*with solemnity*). I know the worst.

MRS. CULVER. I always think that's such a comfort. With closed doors and no one listening to us, so long as a man is kind and civil to his wife, do you blame him very much if he strays occasionally from the narrow path of virtue ?

MARTHA (*rising and moving up to the* R. *end of the sofa*). Do you mean to say that you attach no importance to husbands and wives keeping their marriage vows ?

MRS. CULVER. I think wives should.

BARBARA. But that's grossly unfair. Why should *they* any more than men ?

MRS. CULVER. Because on the whole they like it. We're naturally faithful creatures and we're faithful because we have no particular inclination to be anything else.

BARBARA. I wonder.

(MARTHA *moves slowly across, above the sofa*.)

MRS. CULVER. My dear, you are a widow and perfectly free. Have you really had any great desire to do anything that the world might say you shouldn't ?

BARBARA. I have my business. When you work hard eight hours a day you don't much want to be bothered with love.

MRS. CULVER. A man about the house if often useful. It's nice to have someone around to tell you you're quite right when you know in your heart you're quite wrong.

MARTHA (*to* BARBARA; *turning, below the piano*). By the way, how is your business ?

BARBARA. Growing by leaps and bounds. As a matter of fact I came here today to ask Constance if she would like to come in with me.

MRS. CULVER. Why should she ? John earns plenty of money.

BARBARA. Well, I thought if things came to a crisis she might like to know that her independence was assured.

(MARTHA *moves slowly down* L.C.)

MRS. CULVER. Oh, you want them to come to a crisis, too ?

BARBARA. No, of course I don't. But you know, they can't go on like this. It's a miracle that Constance hasn't heard yet.

MARTHA. I hope she'll find out as quickly as possible. I still think it's mother's duty to tell her.

MRS. CULVER. Which I have no intention of doing.

MARTHA. And if mother won't, I think I ought.

MRS. CULVER. Which I have no intention of permitting.

MARTHA (*moving to* C.). Her position is intolerable. He's humiliated her beyond endurance. I have no words to express my opinion of Marie-Louise, and the first time I see her I shall tell her exactly what I think of her. She's a horrid, ungrateful, mean and contemptible little cat.

BARBARA (*rising, breaking* R., *and turning*).   Anyhow, I think it would be a comfort to Constance to know that if anything happened she ha: me to turn to.

MRS. CULVER.   But John would make her a handsome allowance. He's a very generous man.

MARTHA (*indignantly*).   Do you think Constance would accept it ?

BARBARA (*to below and* R. *of the sofa*).   Martha's quite right, Mrs. Culver.   No woman in those circumstances would take a penny of his money.

MRS. CULVER.   That's what she'd say.   But she'd take care that her lawyer made the best arrangement he could.   Few men know with what ingenuity women can combine the disinterested gesture with an eye for the main chance.

BARBARA (*easing a little, up* R. *of the sofa*).   Aren't you rather cynical, Mrs. Culver ?

MRS. CULVER.   I hope not.   But when women are alone together I don't see why they shouldn't tell the truth now and then.   It's a rest from the weary round of pretending to be something that we quite well know we're not.

MARTHA (*stiffly*).   I'm not aware that I've ever pretended to be anything I wasn't. (*She moves away, down* L.C., *above the low table.*)

MRS. CULVER.   I daresay not, my dear.   But I've always thought you were a little stupid.   You take after your poor father.   Constance and I have the brains of the family.

(CONSTANCE *enters up* L.C. *She is a handsome woman of five and thirty.   She has been out and wears a hat.   She carries a few small packages.*)

BARBARA (*eagerly, crossing above the sofa to* C.).   Constance !

CONSTANCE (*putting her packages on the piano*).   I'm so sorry I wasn't in. (*Moving down.*) How nice of you all to wait.   How are you mother darling ? (*She kisses them—first* BARBARA, *then* MRS. CULVER, *and then* MARTHA.)

MARTHA.   What have you been doing all day, Constance ?

CONSTANCE.   Oh, I've been shopping with Marie-Louise.   She's just coming up.

BARBARA (*with dismay*).   Is she here ?

CONSTANCE (*turning to* BARBARA).   Yes.   She's telephoning.

MARTHA (*ironically*).   You and Marie-Louise are quite inseparable.

CONSTANCE (*crossing to the fireplace*).   I like her.   She amuses me.

(BARBARA *breaks to above the* R. *end of the sofa*.)

MARTHA.   Were you lunching together ?

CONSTANCE (*adjusting an ornament on the mantelpiece*).   No, she was lunching with a young man.

MARTHA (*exchanging a glance with* MRS. CULVER).   Oh, really. (*Breezily.*) John always comes home to luncheon. doesn't he ? (*She eases up to the piano.*)

CONSTANCE (*with great frankness, turning*). When he doesn't have to be at the hospital too early.

MARTHA. Was he lunching with you today?

CONSTANCE (*crossing briskly towards the desk*, L.). No. He was engaged.

MARTHA. Where?

CONSTANCE (*checking at* L.C.). Good heavens, I don't know! (*She moves on to the desk.*) When you've been married as long as I have you never ask your husband where he's going. (*She takes off her gloves.*)

MARTHA (*moving down to the* L. *end of the sofa*). I don't know why not.

CONSTANCE (*smiling*). Because he might take it into his head to ask *you*.

MRS. CULVER. And also because if you're a wise woman you have confidence in your husband.

CONSTANCE. John has never given me a moment's uneasiness.

MARTHA (*moving down* R. *to the easy chair*). You're lucky.

CONSTANCE (*with her tongue in her cheek*). Or wise.

(MARIE-LOUISE *enters up* L.C. *She is a very pretty, beautifully dressed little thing, of the clinging, large-eyed type.*)

MARIE-LOUISE (*moving down* C.). Oh, I didn't know there was a party.

MRS. CULVER (*turning to look at* MARIE-LOUISE). Martha and I are just going.

CONSTANCE. You know my mother, Marie-Louise.

(MRS. CULVER *and* MARIE-LOUISE *exchange a smile of greeting.*)

MARIE-LOUISE. Of course I do.

CONSTANCE. She's a very nice mother.

MRS. CULVER. With her head screwed on the right way and very active for her years.

(MARIE-LOUISE *moves* R., *to* BARBARA.)

MARIE-LOUISE. (*kissing* BARBARA). How are you? (*She moves down and kisses* MARTHA.)

MARTHA. Hallo, darling. (*Looking at her dress.*) That's new, isn't it, Marie Louise?

MARIE-LOUISE. Yes, I've never had it on before.

MARTHA (*sitting, down* R.). Oh, did you put it on because you were lunching with a young man?

MARIE-LOUISE (*above* MARTHA'S *chair*). What makes you think I was lunching with a young man?

MARTHA. Constance told me so.

CONSTANCE (*at the desk*). It was only a guess on my part. (*To* MARIE-LOUISE, *moving in a little*, L.C.) When we met I noticed that your eyes were shining and you had that pleased young look a

woman always gets when someone has been telling her she's the
most adorable thing in the world.

MARTHA. Tell us who it was, Marie-Louise.

CONSTANCE. Do nothing of the kind, Marie-Louise. Keep it
a secret and give us something to gossip about.

BARBARA (*sitting*, R. *of* MRS. CULVER). How is your husband,
dear ?

MARIE-LOUISE (*to the* R. *end of the sofa*). Oh, very well. I've
just been 'phoning him.

BARBARA. I never saw anyone adore his wife so obviously as
he adores you.

MARIE-LOUISE. Yes, he's sweet, isn't he ?

BARBARA. It must be nerve-racking to live up to such devotion.
It would be a dreadful shock if he ever found out that you weren't
everything he thought you.

CONSTANCE (*charmingly*).   But Marie-Louise *is* everything he
thinks her. (*She moves up to the piano.*)

MARIE-LOUSE. And even if I weren't I think it would require
more than the evidence of his eyes to persuade him.

CONSTANCE. Listen. There's John. (*She opens the doors* L.C.
and calls.) John ! John !

JOHN (*off*). Hulloa !

CONSTANCE. Are you coming up ? Marie-Louise is here.

JOHN. Yes, I'm just coming.

CONSTANCE (*closing the doors*).   He's been operating all the
afternoon. (*Moving down* L.C.) I expect he's tired out.

MARTHA (*with a look at* MARIE-LOUISE). I daresay he only had
a sandwich for luncheon.

(JOHN *enters up* C. *He is a tall spare man of about forty.*)

JOHN. Good Lord, I never saw such a lot of people. (*Moving
down* L. *of the sofa.*) How is my mother-in-law ?

MRS. CULVER. Mother-in-lawish.

(JOHN *kisses her, and then turns to* BARBARA.)

JOHN. You know, I only married Constance because her
mother wouldn't have me.

MRS. CULVER. I was too young at the time to marry a boy
twenty years younger than myself.

CONSTANCE (*at* C.; L. *of* JOHN). It hasn't prevented you from
flirting outrageously with the creature ever since.

JOHN. What have you been doing all day, darling ?

CONSTANCE. I've been shopping with Marie-Louise.

JOHN (*crossing below the sofa*). Oh, how do you do ? (*He shakes
hands with* MARIE-LOUISE.) Did you lunch together ?

MARTHA. No, she lunched with a young man.

JOHN. I wish it had been me. (*To* MARIE-LOUISE.) What have
you been doing with yourself lately ? We haven't seen you for ages.

MARIE-LOUISE.   You're never about. Constance and I almost live in one another's pockets.

JOHN.   How's that rich husband of yours ?

MARIE-LOUISE.   I've just been speaking to him. (*Crossing* JOHN *towards* CONSTANCE.) Isn't it a bore, he's got to go down to Birmingham for the night.

CONSTANCE.   You'd better come and dine with us.

MARIE-LOUISE (L. *of the sofa*). Oh, it's awfully nice of you. But I'm tired out. I shall just go to bed and have an egg.

JOHN (*moving up* R.C. *above the sofa*). I was just going to tell you, Constance. I shan't be in this evening. I've got an acute appendix to do.

CONSTANCE.   What a nuisance.

MARTHA.   You've got a wonderful profession, John. If you ever want to do anything or go anywhere you've got an operation and no-one can prove it's a lie.

CONSTANCE (*moving* R. *to the fireplace*). Oh, my dear, you mustn't put suspicions into my innocent head. It would never. occur to John to be deceitful. (*To* JOHN.) Would it ?

JOHN.   I think I'd have to go an awful long way before I managed to deceive you, darling.

CONSTANCE (*with a little smile*). Sometimes I think you're right.

MARIE-LOUISE.   I do like to see a husband and wife so devoted to one another as you and John. You've been married fifteen years, haven't you ?

JOHN.   Yes. And it doesn't seem a day too much.

MARIE-LOUISE.   Well, I must be running along. I'm late already. (*Moving towards the doors.*) Good-bye darling. Good-bye, Mrs. Culver.

(JOHN *goes up to the doors.*)

CONSTANCE.   Good-bye, darling.   We've had such a nice afternoon.

MARIE-LOUISE (*giving her hand to* JOHN). Good-bye.

JOHN (*opening the door*). Oh, I'll come downstairs with you.

MARTHA (*rising*). I was just going, Marie-Louise. I'll come with you.

MARIE-LOUISE (*with presence of mind*). John, I wonder if you'd mind looking at my knee for a minute ? It's been rather painful for the last day or two.

JOHN.   Of course not. Come into my consulting-room. (*Moving to the door up* R. *with* MARIE-LOUISE.) These knee-caps are trouble-some things when you once get them out of order.

MARTHA (*firmly, as she crosses above the sofa, to* C.). I'll wait for you. You won't be long, will you ? (*Turning to look at* MARIE-LOUISE.) We might share a taxi.

MARIE-LOUISE.   I've got my car.

MARTHA.   Oh, how nice ! You can give me a lift then.

MARIE-LOUISE.   Of course. I shall be delighted.

(JOHN *opens the door for* MARIE-LOUISE. *She exits and he follows her.* CONSTANCE *has watched this little scene coolly but with an alert mind from the fireplace.*)

MARTHA (*moving down,* L. *of the sofa*). What is the matter with her knee ?
CONSTANCE. It slips.
MARTHA. What happens then ?
CONSTANCE. She slips too.
MARTHA. Are you never jealous of these women who come and see John in his consulting-room ?
CONSTANCE. He always has a nurse within call in case they should attempt to take liberties with him.
MARTHA (*amiably*). Is the nurse there now ?
CONSTANCE. And anyway I can't help thinking that the sort of woman who wants to be made love to in a consulting-room with a lively odour of antiseptics, is the sort of woman who wears horrid undies. I could never bring myself to be jealous of her.
MARTHA (*moving away to the low table,* L.C.). Marie-Louise gave me two of hers to copy only the other day.
CONSTANCE (*crossing up to the piano*). I thought them sweet. Did she give you the black chiffon one ? I've copied that. (*She begins to open a package.*)
BARBARA (*rising and easing to the fireplace*). It's true that Marie-Louise is very pretty. (*She adjusts her hat at the mirror.*)
CONSTANCE. Marie-Louise is a darling. But she and John have known each other far too long. John likes her, of course, but he says she has no brain.
MARTHA (*moving to the chair down* L.). Men don't always say what they think. (*She sits.*)
CONSTANCE. Fortunately, or we shouldn't always know what they feel.

(BARBARA *has turned to listen.*)

MARTHA. Don't you think John has *any* secrets from you ?
CONSTANCE (*as she crosses* L. *to the desk with her parcel, wrapping and string*). My dear, you talk like a confirmed spinster. Do you really think that men are mysterious ? They're children. (*Crossing back to the piano.*) Why, my dear, John at forty isn't nearly so grown up as Helen at fourteen.
BARBARA (*sitting in the chair down* R.). How is your girl, Constance ?
CONSTANCE. Oh, she's very well. (*She sits on the piano stool.*) She loves boarding-school, you know. They're like little boys, men. Sometimes, of course, they're rather naughty and you have to pretend to be angry with them. They attach so much importance to such entirely unimportant things that it's really touching. And they're so helpless. Just like dogs. They haven't got the sense to come in out of the rain, poor darlings. You can't help liking them.

I think they're sweet, but it's absurd to take them seriously. You're a wise woman, mother. What do you think ?

MRS. CULVER. I think you're not in love with your husband.

CONSTANCE. What nonsense.

(JOHN *enters* R.)

.JOHN. Marie-Louise is waiting for you, Martha. (*As* MARTHA *rises and crosses to up* C.) I've just put a little bandage round her knee.

CONSTANCE. I hope you weren't rough.

MARTHA (*turning to* CONSTANCE). Good-bye, dear. (*Turning to* MRS. CULVER.) Are you coming, mother ?

MRS. CULVER. Not just yet.

MARTHA. Oh. (*After a slight hesitation.*) Good-bye, Barbara.

(MARTHA *and* JOHN *go out up* C.)

BARBARA (*rising and crossing to* R. *of* CONSTANCE, *at the piano stool*). Constance, I've got a suggestion to make to you. You know that my business has been growing by leaps and bounds and I simply cannot get along alone any more. I was wondering if you'd like to come in with me.

CONSTANCE. Oh, my dear, I'm not a business woman.

BARBARA. You've got marvellous taste and you have ideas. You could do all the decorating and I'd confine myself to buying and selling furniture.

CONSTANCE. But, I've got no capital.

BARBARA. I've got all the capital I want. I must have *help* and I know no-one more suitable than you. We'd go fifty-fifty and I think I car. promise that you'd make a thousand to fifteen hundred a year.

CONSTANCE. I've been an idle woman so long. I think I'd find it dreadfully hard to work eight hours a day.

BARBARA. Won't you think it over ? It's very interesting, you know. You're naturally energetic. Don't you get bored with doing nothing all the time ?

CONSTANCE. I don't think John would like it. After all, it would look as though he couldn't afford to support me.

BARBARA. Oh, but nowadays plenty of women have careers, just as men do.

CONSTANCE. I think my career is looking after John—running his house for him, and making him happy and comfortable.

BARBARA. Don't you think it rather a mistake to put all your eggs in one basket ?

(MRS. CULVER *rises, breaks to the fireplace and is apparently admiring something on the mantelpiece.* BARBARA *glances at her and then turns again to* CONSTANCE.)

Independence is a very good thing, and a woman who stands on her own feet can look to the future with a good deal of confidence.

CONSTANCE. It's sweet of you, but so long as John and I are happy together I think I should be foolish to do anything to vex him.

BARBARA. Well, I want you to know that if you change your mind the job is open to you.

CONSTANCE. Don't think me horrid if I say I hope I shall never need to accept it.

BARBARA. Of course not. But you've only to say the word.

(MRS. CULVER *turns and eases to below the sofa.*)

Good-bye, darling.

CONSTANCE. Good-bye, dear.

(*They kiss.*)

BARBARA. Good-bye, Mrs. Culver.

MRS. CULVER. Good-bye.

(CONSTANCE *and* BARBARA *go up to the doors.* BARBARA *exits.* CONSTANCE *rings the bell near the doors, returns to the piano, and deals with another parcel.*)

MRS. CULVER. Are you quite happy, dear ?

CONSTANCE. Oh, quite. Don't I look it ?

MRS. CULVER. I'm bound to say you do. So far as I can judge by the look of you, I should say you haven't a trouble in the world.

CONSTANCE. You'd be wrong. My cook has given notice and she makes the best meringues I've ever eaten.

(MRS. CULVER *sits at the* R. *end of the sofa.*)

MRS. CULVER. I like John.

CONSTANCE. So do I. (*Carrying the package and string to the desk* L.) He has all the solid qualities that make a man a good husband; an agreeable temper, a sense of humour, and an entire indifference to petty extravagance.

MRS. CULVER. How right you are, darling, to realise that those *are* the solid qualities. Of course, one has to compromise in life. If one wants to be happy in one's own way, one must let others be happy in theirs. The great thing is not to let vanity warp one's reasonable point of view.

CONSTANCE (*in humorous reproof*). Mother, mother, pull yourself together !

MRS. CULVER. Everybody's so clever nowadays. They see everything but the obvious. I've discovered that I only have to say it quite simply in order to be thought a most original and amusing old lady.

CONSTANCE (*easing to the low table* L.). Spare me, darling. (*She picks up a book and examines it.*)

MRS. CULVER (*affectionately*). If at any time anything went wrong with you, you would tell your mother, wouldn't you ?

CONSTANCE (*putting down the book*). Of course. (*She moves slowly towards the sofa.*)

MRS. CULVER. I hate the thought that you might be unhappy and let a foolish pride prevent you from letting me console and advise you.

CONSTANCE (*sitting on the* L. *arm of the sofa: with feeling*). It wouldn't, mother dear.

MRS. CULVER. I had rather an odd experience the other day. A little friend of mine came to see me, and told me that her husband was neglecting her.

CONSTANCE. Oh, well, John never neglects me.

MRS. CULVER. I asked her why she told me, and not her own mother. She said that her mother never wanted her to marry, and it would mortify her now to have to say she had made a mistake. Of course, I gave her a good talking to. She didn't get much sympathy from me.

CONSTANCE (*with a smile*). That was very unkind, wasn't it ?

MRS. CULVER. I have my own ideas about marriage. If a man neglects his wife it's her own fault, and if he's systematically unfaithful to her, in nine cases out of ten she only has herself to blame.

CONSTANCE (*rising and going up to the bell push*). Systematically is a grim word. (*She rings the bell.*)

MRS. CULVER. No sensible woman attaches importance to an occasional slip. Time and chance are responsible for that.

CONSTANCE (*moving down* C.). And shall we say, masculine vanity ?

MRS. CULVER. I told my little friend that if her husband was unfaithful to her it was because he found other women more attractive. Why should she be angry with him for that ? Her business was to be more attractive than they.

CONSTANCE. You are not what they call a feminist, mother, are you ?

MRS. CULVER. After all, what is fidelity ?

CONSTANCE (*turning and crossing* L. *to the window*). Mother, do you mind if I open the window ?

MRS. CULVER. It is open.

CONSTANCE. In that case, do you mind if I shut it ? (*She shuts the window.*) I feel that when a woman of your age asks such a question I should make some sort of symbolic gesture. (*She moves to* R. *of the low table* L.C.)

MRS. CULVER. Don't be ridiculous. Of course I believe in fidelity for women. I suppose no one has ever questioned the desirability of that. But men are different. Women should remember that they have their homes and their name and position and their family, and they should learn to close their eyes when it's possible they may see something they are not meant to.

(BENTLEY *enters up* L.C.)

BENTLEY. Did you ring, madam ?

B

CONSTANCE. Yes. I am expecting Mr. Bernard Kersal. I'm not at home to anybody else.

BENTLEY. Very good, madam.

CONSTANCE. Is Mr. Middleton in ?

BENTLEY. Yes, Madam, he's in the consulting room.

CONSTANCE. Very well.

(BENTLEY exits.)

MRS. CULVER. Is that a polite way of telling me that I had better take myself off ?

CONSTANCE (*moving towards* C.). Of course not. On the contrary, I particularly want you to stay. (*She sits on the* L. *arm of the sofa.*)

MRS. CULVER. Who is this mysterious gentleman ?

CONSTANCE. Mother ! *Bernard.*

MRS. CULVER. That says nothing to me at all. Not Saint Bernard, darling ?

CONSTANCE. Pull yourself together, my pet. You must remember Bernard Kersal. He proposed to me.

MRS. CULVER. Oh, my dear, you cannot expect me to remember the names of all the young men who proposed to you.

CONSTANCE. Yes, but he proposed more than any of the others.

MRS. CULVER. Why ?

CONSTANCE. I suppose because I refused him. (*Rising and moving to* L.C.) I can't think of any other reason.

MRS. CULVER. He made no impression on me.

CONSTANCE (*turning*). I very nearly married him, you know.

MRS. CULVER. Why didn't you ?

CONSTANCE (*moving to the* L. *end of the sofa*). I think he was a trifle too much inclined to lie down on the floor and let me walk over him.

MRS. CULVER. In short, he had no sense of humour.

CONSTANCE. I was quite certain that he loved me, and I was never absolutely sure that John did.

MRS. CULVER. Well, you're sure now, dear, aren't you ?

CONSTANCE. Oh yes. John adores me.

MRS. CULVER. And what's this young man coming for today ?

CONSTANCE. He's not such a very young man any more. He was twenty-nine then and so he must be nearly forty-five now.

MRS. CULVER. He isn't still in love with you ?

CONSTANCE (*crossing to the desk*). I shouldn't think so. (*Taking her mirror from her handbag and looking at her hair.*) Do you think it possible after fifteen years ? It's surely very unlikely. (*Glancing across at* MRS. CULVER.) Don't look at me like that, mother. I don't like it.

MRS. CULVER. Don't talk stuff and nonsense to me, child. Of course you know if he's in love with you or not.

CONSTANCE (*putting away her mirror*). But I haven't seen him since I married John. (*To* L. *of the low table.*) You see he lives in

China. He's a merchant or something in Shanghai. (*Moving to* C.)
He came when I was so dreadfully ill and I didn't see him.

MRS. CULVER.   Oh ! Why's he here now then ? Have you been
corresponding with him ?

CONSTANCE.   No. (*Moving up to the piano.*) One can't write
letters to anyone one never sees for fifteen years. (*Looking through
some music.*) He always sends me flowers on my birthday.

MRS. CULVER.   That's rather sweet of him.

CONSTANCE (*turning*).   And the other day, I had a letter from
him saying he was in England, and would like to see me. (*Putting
down the music.*) So I asked him to come today. (*She moves across
R. above the sofa.*)

MRS. CULVER.   I wondered why you were so smart.

CONSTANCE (*moving down* R. *to the fireplace*).   Of course he may
be terribly changed. Men go off so dreadfully, don't they ? He may
be bald and fat now.

MRS. CULVER.   He may be married.

CONSTANCE (*turning*).   Oh, if he were I don't think he'd want to
come and see me would he ?

MRS. CULVER.   I see you're under the impression that he's still
in love with you.

CONSTANCE (*crossing* C., *below the sofa*).   Oh, I'm not.

MRS. CULVER.   Then why are you so nervous ?

CONSTANCE (*turning and sitting on the* L. *arm of the settee*).   It's
only natural that I shouldn't want him to think me old and haggard.
He adored me, mother. I suppose he still thinks of me as I was then.
It wouldn't be very nice if his face fell about a yard and a half when
he came into the room.

MRS. CULVER (*rising*).   I think I'd much better leave you to face
the ordeal alone.

CONSTANCE.   Oh, no, mother, you must stay. I particularly
want you. You see, he may be awful, and I may wish I'd never seen
him again. It'll be so much easier if you're here. I may not want
to be alone with him at all.

MRS. CULVER.   Oh. (*She sits again, at the* R. *end of the sofa.*)

CONSTANCE (*with a twinkle in her eye*).   On the other hand, I may.

MRS. CULVER.   It seems to me you're putting me in a slightly
embarrassing situation.

CONSTANCE (*rising from the arm of the sofa and sitting* L. *of*
MRS. CULVER).   Now listen. If I think he's awful, we'll just talk
about the weather for a few minutes and then we'll have an ominous
pause and stare at him. That always makes a man feel a perfect
fool and the moment a man feels a fool, he gets up and goes.

MRS. CULVER.   Sometimes they don't know how to, poor dears,
and the earth will never open and swallow them up.

CONSTANCE.   On the other hand if I think he looks rather nice,
I shall just take out my handkerchief and carelessly place it on the
piano.

MRS. CULVER.   Why ?

CONSTANCE (*rising*). Darling, in order that you may rise to your aged feet and say, well, you really must be running along. (*She turns up to the piano.*)

MRS. CULVER. Yes, I know that, but why should you carelessly place your handkerchief on the piano ?

CONSTANCE (*turning, at up* L.C.). Because I am a creature of impulse. I shall have an impulse to place my handkerchief on the piano. (*She goes to the piano for her bag.*)

MRS. CULVER. Oh, very well. But I always mistrust impulses.

(BENTLEY *enters up* L.C.)

BENTLEY. Mr. Kersal.

(BERNARD KERSAL *enters. He is a tall good-looking man, sunburned and of healthy appearance. He is evidently very fit and he carries his forty-six years well.* BENTLEY *exits.*)

CONSTANCE (*meeting* BERNARD *up* C. *and shaking hands*). How do you do. Do you remember my mother ? (*She brings* BERNARD *down stage.*)

BERNARD (*moving down to* MRS. CULVER *and shaking hands with her*). I'm sure she doesn't remember me.

(CONSTANCE *takes a small handkerchief out of her bag.* MRS. CULVER *observes this.*)

MRS. CULVER. That is the soft answer that turneth away wrath.

CONSTANCE. It's rather late for tea, isn't it ? Would you like a drink ? (*As she says this she goes* L. *and places her handkerchief on the piano.*)

BERNARD. No, thanks. I've just this moment had one.

CONSTANCE. To brace you for seeing me ?

BERNARD. I was nervous.

CONSTANCE (*moving down again*). Have I changed as much as you expected ?

BERNARD. Oh, that's not what I was nervous about.

MRS. CULVER (*with a gesture inviting him to sit*). Is it really fifteen years since you saw Constance ?

BERNARD. Yes. (*He sits* L. *of* MRS. CULVER.) I didn't see her when I was last in England. I had to go out to China again and get my business together. I haven't had a chance to come home before.

(CONSTANCE *has been giving her mother significant looks, but her mother does not notice them.* CONSTANCE *takes a second handkerchief out of her bag.*)

MRS. CULVER. And are you home for long ?

BERNARD. A year.

MRS. CULVER. Have you brought your wife with you ?

BERNARD. I'm not married.

MRS. CULVER. Oh, Constance said you were married to a Chinese lady.

CONSTANCE. Nonsense, mother. (*She gives the handkerchief a tiny flourish.*) I never said anything of the sort. (*She goes to the table and puts the handkerchief down.*)

MRS. CULVER. Oh, perhaps I was thinking of Julia Linton. She married an Egyptian pasha. I believe she's very happy. At all events he hasn't killed her yet.

(CONSTANCE *returns to* C.)

BERNARD (*to* CONSTANCE). How is your husband?

CONSTANCE. He's very well. I daresay he'll be in presently.

BERNARD. Haven't you got a little sister? I suppose she's come out by now?

MRS. CULVER. He means Martha. She's come out and gone in again.

CONSTANCE (*crossing down* R.). She was not so very much younger than me, you know.

(MRS. CULVER *has taken no notice of the handkerchiefs and in desperation* CONSTANCE *takes a third from her bag.*)

MRS. CULVER. Do you like the East, Mr. Kersal?

BERNARD. One has a pretty good time there, you know.

(CONSTANCE *crosses* L., *to the low table displaying the third handkerchief.*)

CONSTANCE (*as she crosses*). Would you like to smoke? There are some cigarettes here.

(*She puts the handkerchief down ostentatiously and picks up the cigarette box. Now* MRS. CULVER *sees the three handkerchiefs and starts.*)

MRS. CULVER (*rising*). I wonder what the time is?

CONSTANCE (*putting the cigarette box on the table*). It's late, mother. Are you dining out tonight? I suppose you want to have a lie down before you dress for dinner.

(BERNARD *rises.*)

MRS. CULVER. I hope I shall see you again, Mr. Kersal.

(*They shake hands.*)

BERNARD. Thank you very much.

(MRS. CULVER *crosses to up* C. CONSTANCE *accompanies her to the door.* BERNARD *eases to the fireplace.*)

MRS. CULVER. Good-bye, darling. (*In a whisper.*) I couldn't remember if the handkerchiefs meant go or stay.

CONSTANCE. You had only to use your eyes.

MRS. CULVER.   You only confused me by putting more and more handkerchiefs on the piano.

CONSTANCE (*in an undertone*).   For goodness sake, go, mother. (*Aloud.*)   Good-bye, my sweet.   I'm sorry you've got to run away so soon.

MRS. CULVER.   Good-bye.

(*She exits.* CONSTANCE *closes the doors and moves down* C.)

CONSTANCE (*as she crosses down*).   Did you think it was very rude of us to whisper ?   Mother has a passion for secrets.

BERNARD (*coming below the* R. *end of the sofa*).   Of course not.

CONSTANCE.   Now, let's sit down and make ourselves comfortable.   Let me look at you.

(BERNARD *turns.*)

You haven't changed much.   You're a little thinner, and perhaps a little more lined. (*Crossing to the low table.*)   Men are so lucky— if they have any character they grow better-looking as they grow older. (*Bringing the cigarettes to* R.C.)   Do you know I'm thirty-five now ?

BERNARD.   What does that matter ?

CONSTANCE (*below the sofa, offering cigarettes*).   Shall I tell you something ?   (BERNARD *takes a cigarette ; she returns with the box* L.)   When you wrote and suggested coming here, I was delighted at the thought of seeing you again, and wrote at once. (*Putting the box down and moving back to below the sofa with an ashtray.*)   And then I was panic-stricken.   I would have given almost anything not to have sent that letter.   And all today I've had such a horrible feeling at the pit of my stomach.   Didn't you see my knees wobble when you came into the room ? (*She sits.*)

BERNARD.   In God's name, why ? (*He sits* R. *of* CONSTANCE.)

CONSTANCE.   I should be a perfect fool if I didn't know that when I was a girl I was very pretty.   It's rather a pang when you are forced to the conclusion that you're not quite so pretty as you were. People don't tell one.   One tries to hide it from oneself.   Anyhow I thought I'd rather know the worst.   That's one of the reasons I asked you to come.

BERNARD.   Whatever I thought you can hardly imagine that I should be deliberately rude.

CONSTANCE.   Of course not.   But I watched your face.   I was afraid I'd see there : " By God, how she's gone off."

BERNARD.   And did you ?

CONSTANCE.   You were rather shy when you came in.   You weren't thinking of me.

BERNARD.   It's quite true—years ago you were a pretty girl. Now, you're lovely.   You're ten times more beautiful than you were then.

CONSTANCE.   It's nice of you to say so.

BERNARD.   Don't you believe it ?

CONSTANCE. I think *you* do. And I confess that's sufficiently gratifying. Now tell me, why aren't you married ? It's time you did, you know, or it'll be too late. You'll have a very lonely old age if you don't.

BERNARD. I never wanted to marry anyone but you.

CONSTANCE. Oh, come, you're not going to tell me that you've never been in love since you were in love with me ?

BERNARD. No, I've been in love half a dozen times, but when it came to the point I found I still loved you best.

CONSTANCE. I like you for saying that. I shouldn't have believed it if you'd said you'd never loved anybody else, and I should have been vexed with you for thinking me such a fool as to believe it.

BERNARD. You see, it was you I loved in the others. One because she had hair like yours, and another because her smile reminded me of your smile.

CONSTANCE (*putting her hand lightly on his arm*). I hate to think that I've made you unhappy. (*She withdraws her hand.*)

BERNARD. But you haven't. I've had a very good time ; I've enjoyed my work ; I've made a bit of money and I've had a lot of fun. I don't blame you for having married John instead of me.

CONSTANCE. Do you remember John ?

BERNARD. Of course I do. He was a very nice fellow. I daresay he's made you a better husband than I should have. I've had my ups and downs. I'm very irritable sometimes. John's been able to give you everything you wanted. You were much safer with him. By the way, I suppose I can still call you Constance ?

CONSTANCE. Of course. Why not ? Do you know, I think you have a very nice nature, Bernard.

BERNARD. Are you happy with John ?

CONSTANCE. Oh very. I think I can quite honestly say that ours has been a very happy and successful marriage.

BERNARD. I'm awfully glad to hear that. Do you think it's cheek to ask if John loves you ?

CONSTANCE. I'm sure he loves me.

BERNARD (*stubbing out his cigarette on the ashtray*). And you love him ?

CONSTANCE. Very much.

BERNARD (*rising*). May I make a short speech ?

CONSTANCE. If I may interrupt at suitable moments.

BERNARD (*moving below the sofa, to* C.). I hope you're going to let me see a great deal of you during this year I've got at home. (*He turns.*)

CONSTANCE (*turning to look at him*). *I* want to see a great deal of *you*.

BERNARD (*at* C.). There's just one thing I want to get off my chest, and then I needn't refer to it again. I am just as madly in love with you as I was when I asked you to marry me, fifteen years ago. I think I shall remain in love with you all my life. I'm too old a dog to learn new tricks. But I want you to know that you needn't have the smallest fear that I shall make a nuisance of myself.

CONSTANCE (*after a tiny pause; rising*).   That's not such a very
long speech after all.   (*Taking the ashtray to the small table* R.,
above the fireplace.)   At a public dinner they would hardly even call
it a few remarks. (*She turns and eases to below the* R. *end of the sofa*.)
    BERNARD.   All I ask for is your friendship and if in return I
care to give you my love I don't see that it's anyone's business
but my own.
    CONSTANCE.   I don't think it is.   (*Moving in a pace*.)   I think I
can be a very good friend, Bernard.

(*The doors up* L.C. *open and* JOHN *enters*.)

    JOHN.   Oh, I'm sorry.   I didn't know you were engaged.
    CONSTANCE.   I'm not.   Come in.   This is Bernard Kersal.
    JOHN (*who has moved down* C.).   How do you do ?
    BERNARD.   I'm afraid you don't remember me.
    JOHN.   If you ask me point-blank, I think it's safer to confess
I don't.
    CONSTANCE.   Don't be so silly, John.   He used to come to
mother's.
    JOHN.   Before we were married, d'you mean ?
    CONSTANCE.   Yes.   You both spent several week-ends with us
together.
    JOHN (*to* CONSTANCE).   My dear, that was fifteen years ago.
(*To* BERNARD.)   I'm awfully sorry not to remember you, but I'm
delighted to see you now.

(*They shake hands*.)

    CONSTANCE.   He's just come back from China.
    JOHN (*moving a little* L.).   Oh, well, I hope we shall see you again.
(*Checking and turning to* CONSTANCE.)   I'm just going along to the
club to have a rubber before dinner, darling. (*To* BERNARD.)   Why
don't you dine here with Constance ?   I've got an acute appendix
and she'll be all alone, poor darling.
    BERNARD.   Oh, that's awfully kind of you.
    CONSTANCE.   It would be a friendly act.   Are you free ?
    BERNARD (*smiling*).   Always, to do a friendly act.
    CONSTANCE (*putting out her hand*).   Very well.   I shall expect you
at eight-fifteen.

CURTAIN.

ACT II

SCENE: *The same. Late afternoon, a fortnight later.*

When the CURTAIN *rises,* MARTHA, *in walking costume and a hat, is seated down* L., *looking at an illustrated paper.* BENTLEY *enters up* C.

BENTLEY. Mr. Kersal is here, miss.
MARTHA. Oh ! Ask him to come up.
BENTLEY. Very good, miss.

(*He exits.* MARTHA *rises, takes the paper to the desk* L., *puts it down, and returns to* L.C. *as* BENTLEY *enters, followed by* BERNARD.)

Mr. Kersal.

(*He exits.* BERNARD *moves down towards* MARTHA.)

MARTHA (*as they shake hands*). Constance is dressing. She won't be very long.
BERNARD. Oh, I see. (*He breaks a little* R.C.) Well, there's no violent hurry.
MARTHA (*moving to the piano*). You're taking her to Wimbledon, aren't you ?
BERNARD. That was the idea. I know some of the fellows who are playing today.
MARTHA (*looking at some music on the piano*). Are you having a good time in London ?
BERNARD. Marvellous. When a man's lived in the East as long as I have, he's apt to feel rather out of it when he comes home. But Constance and John have been very good to me.
MARTHA (*putting aside the music*). Do you like John ?
BERNARD (*breaking* R., *below the sofa*). Yes. He's been awfully kind.
MARTHA (*moving to* C.). Do you know, I remember you quite well.
BERNARD (*offering her a cigarette*). Oh, you can't.
MARTHA (*taking the cigarette*). You were madly in love with Constance in those days, weren't you ?
BERNARD (*lighting her cigarette, and then one for himself*). You know, it's so long ago I forget.
MARTHA. You're in love with her still, aren't you ?
BERNARD. Not a bit.
MARTHA. Upon my soul, you've got a nerve. (*Turning up stage,* L. *of the sofa.*) Why, you donkey, you're giving it away all the time. Do you know what you look like when she's in the room ?
BERNARD. I thought you were an odious child when you were sixteen, Martha, and now that you're thirty-two I think you're a horrible woman. (*He turns away to the fireplace.*)

25

MARTHA. I'm not really. (*She eases below the* L. *arm of the sofa.*) But I'm very fond of Constance and I'm inclined to be rather fond of you.

BERNARD (*turning to face her*). Don't you think you could show your attachment by minding your own business ?

MARTHA (*sitting down on the* L. *arm of the sofa*). Why does it make you angry because I've told you that no one can see you with Constance for five minutes without knowing that you adore her ?

BERNARD. My dear, I'm here for one year. I want to be happy. I don't want to give trouble or cause trouble. I value my friendship with Constance and I hate the idea that anything should interfere with it.

MARTHA. Hasn't it occurred to you that she may want more than your friendship ?

BERNARD (*sharply, breaking to below the* R. *end of the sofa*). No, it has *not* !

MARTHA. You need not jump down my throat.

BERNARD (*coldly*). Constance is perfectly happy with her husband.

(MARTHA *regards him with a faint contemptuous smile. He crosses* L., *below her, in silence.*)

MARTHA. You poor fool, don't you know that John has been notoriously unfaithful to Constance for ages ?

(BERNARD *turns sharply and stares at her for a moment.*)

BERNARD (*moving in, to* L.C.). I don't believe it.

MARTHA (*standing*). Ask anyone you like. Mother knows it. Barbara Fawcett knows it. Everyone knows it but Constance.

BERNARD. That certainly isn't true. Mrs. Durham told me when I met her at dinner two or three days ago, that John and Constance were the most devoted couple she'd ever known.

MARTA. Did Marie-Louise tell you that ?

BERNARD. She did.

(MARTHA *begins to laugh. She can hardly restrain herself.*)

MARTHA (*breaking* R. *towards the fireplace*). The nerve. Marie-Louise ! (*Turning.*) Oh, my poor Bernard. Marie-Louise is John's mistress.

BERNARD. She is Constance's greatest friend.

MARTHA. Yes.

BERNARD (*moving to the* L. *end of the sofa*). If this is a pack of lies I swear I'll damned well wring your neck.

MARTHA. All right.

BERNARD (*turning and breaking* L.C.). That was a silly thing to say. I'm sorry. (*He stands* R. *of the low table* L.)

MARTHA. Oh, I don't mind. I like a man to be violent. I think you're just the sort of man Constance needs.

BERNARD (*turning sharply*). What the devil do you mean by that ?

MARTHA. It can't go on. (*Easing to the* L. *end of the sofa.*) Constance is being made perfectly ridiculous. (*Sitting on the arm of the sofa.*) I thought she ought to be told and as everyone else seemed to shirk the job I was prepared to do it myself. My mother was so disagreeable about it, I've had to promise not to say a word.

BERNARD (*moving a little towards* C.). You're not under the delusion that I'm going to tell her ?

MARTHA. No, I don't really think it would come very well from you. But things can't go on. She's bound to find out. All I want you to do is to . . . well, stand by.

BERNARD. But Marie-Louise has got a husband. What about him ?

MARTHA. His only ambition in life is to make a million. He's the sort of fool who thinks a woman loves him just because he loves her. Marie-Louise can turn him round her little finger.

BERNARD. Has Constance never suspected ?

MARTHA. Never. You've only got to look at her. Really, her self-confidence sometimes is positively maddening.

BERNARD (*slightly turned away*). I wonder if it wouldn't be better that she never did find out. She's so happy.

MARTHA. I thought you loved her.

BERNARD. Enough to want her happiness above all things.

MARTHA (*rising slowly and moving to above the sofa*). You *are* forty-five aren't you ? I forgot that for a moment.

BERNARD (*looking at her*). Dear Martha. You have such an attractive way of putting things. (*He moves away* L.)

CONSTANCE (*off*). Bentley ! Bentley !

MARTHA. Oh, there's Constance. I can't imagine where mother is. (*Moving towards the door up* R.) I think I'll go into the brown room and write a letter.

(*She exits.* BERNARD *is staring out of the window. He makes no movement when* MARTHA *goes out. A moment later* CONSTANCE *enters up* C. BERNARD *turns.*)

CONSTANCE. Have I kept you waiting ?

BERNARD (*moving to* I.C.). It doesn't matter.

CONSTANCE (*moving down*). Hulloa ! What's up ?

BERNARD. With me ? Nothing. Why ?

CONSTANCE. You look all funny. Why are your eyes suddenly opaque ?

BERNARD. I didn't know they were.

CONSTANCE. Are you trying to hide something from me ?

BERNARD. Of course not.

CONSTANCE (*easing away above the sofa*). I hate people who keep secrets from me.

BERNARD (*to* C.). I have no secrets from you.

CONSTANCE (*turning—with sudden suspicion*). Wasn't Martha here when you came ? She hasn't gone, has she ?

BERNARD. She's waiting for her mother. She's gone into another room to write letters.

CONSTANCE. Did you see her?

BERNARD (*trying to be very casual, strolling down* R. *towards the fireplace*). Yes. We had a little chat about the weather.

CONSTANCE (*looking at his back and immediately grasping what has happened*). Oh! Don't you think we ought to be starting?

BERNARD. There's plenty of time. (*Turning.*) It's no good getting there too early.

CONSTANCE (*moving up* L.). Then I'll take off my hat. (*She puts her hat and bag on the piano.*)

BERNARD (*below the* R. *end of the sofa*). It's jolly here, isn't it? I love your room.

CONSTANCE (*moving towards the sofa*). Do you like it? I did it myself. Barbara Fawcett wants me to go into the decorating business. She's in it, you know, and she's making quite a lot of money.

BERNARD (*smiling to hide his anxiety in asking the question*). Aren't you happy at home?

CONSTANCE (*breezily*). I don't think it necessarily means one's unhappy at home because one wants an occupation. (*She sits at the* L. *end of the sofa.*) But as a matter of fact I refused Barbara's offer.

BERNARD (*insisting*). You are happy, aren't you?

CONSTANCE. Very.

BERNARD. You've made *me* very happy during this last fortnight.

CONSTANCE. I'm very glad you think so. I don't know that I've done anything very much for you.

BERNARD. Yes, you have. (*He sits on her* R.) You've let me see you.

CONSTANCE (*smiling*). I let the policeman at the corner do that, you know.

BERNARD. You mustn't think that because I take care only to talk to you of quite casual things, I don't still love you with all my heart.

CONSTANCE (*quite coolly*). We agreed when first you came back that your feelings were entirely your business.

BERNARD. Do you mind my loving you?

CONSTANCE. Oughtn't we all to love one another?

BERNARD. Don't make fun of me!

CONSTANCE. My dear, I can't help being pleased and flattered and rather touched. It is rather wonderful that anyone should care for me . . .

BERNARD (*interrupting*). So much—— ?

CONSTANCE. After so many years.

BERNARD (*leaning towards her*). But my dear . . .

CONSTANCE (*going on with her own speech*). But I don't in the least want you to make love to me now.

BERNARD (*sitting back*). I know. I'm not going to.

CONSTANCE (*amused and a trifle taken aback*). I don't quite know what you've been doing for the last five minutes.
BERNARD. I was merely stating a few plain-facts.
CONSTANCE. Oh, I beg your pardon. I thought it was something quite different.
BERNARD. I've been very good during the last fortnight, haven't I ?
CONSTANCE. Yes, I kept on saying to myself, I wonder if a pat. of butter really would melt in his mouth.
BERNARD. Well, for just a minute I'm going to let myself go.
CONSTANCE. I wouldn't if I were you.
BERNARD. Yes, but you're not. I want to tell you—just once—that there's never been anyone in the world for me but you.
CONSTANCE. Oh, nonsense. There have been half-a-dozen.
BERNARD. They were all you. I love you with all my heart. I want you to know that if ever you're in trouble I should look upon it as the greatest possible happiness to be allowed to help you.
CONSTANCE. It's sweet of you to say so.
BERNARD. Don't you believe it ?
CONSTANCE (*with a charming smile*). Yes. (*She rises.*)
BERNARD (*looking up at her*). I should like to think that it meant —oh, not very much, but just a little to you.
CONSTANCE (*almost shaken*). It means a great deal. (*Moving down R.*) Thank you.
BERNARD (*rising*). Now we won't say anything more about it.
CONSTANCE (*turning; recovering her accustomed coolness*). But why did you think it necessary to say all this just now ?
BERNARD (*moving away,* L. *of the sofa*). I wanted to get it off my chest.
CONSTANCE. Oh, really.
BERNARD (*turning, above and* L. *of the sofa*). You're not angry with me ?
CONSTANCE. Oh, Bernard, I'm not that kind of a fool at all . . . It's a pity that Martha doesn't marry.
BERNARD. Don't think that I'm going to marry her.
CONSTANCE. I don't. (*Crossing to* L.C.) I merely thought that a husband would be a pleasant and useful occupation for her. (*Turning.*) She's quite a nice girl, you know. A liar, of course, but otherwise all right.
BERNARD. Oh ?
CONSTANCE. Yes, a terrible liar, even for a woman . . . Shall we start now ? (*Going to the piano.*) It's no good getting there when it's all over.
BERNARD. All right. Let's start.
CONSTANCE. I'll put my hat on again. (*Crossing to the doors up* C.) I shall only be a minute.

(*She exits. BERNARD stands above the* L. *end of the sofa, thoughtful. A moment later BENTLEY enters up* C., *and ushers in MARIE-LOUISE. BERNARD turns.*)

MARIE-LOUISE (*to* BERNARD; *a little startled*). Oh, how do you do ? (*To* BENTLEY.) Will you tell Mr. Middleton at once ?

BENTLEY. Yes, Madam.

(*Exit* BENTLEY.)

MARIE-LOUISE (*rather flustered*). I particularly wanted to see John for a minute and there are patients waiting to see him, so I asked Bentley if he couldn't come here. (*She moves down* L.C.)

BERNARD. I'll take myself off.

MARIE-LOUISE. I'm awfully sorry, but it's rather urgent. John hates to be disturbed like this.

BERNARD. I'll go into the next room. (*He crosses to the door* R.)

MARIE-LOUISE. Are you waiting for Constance ?

BERNARD (*turning at the door*). Yes, I'm taking her to Wimbledon. She's putting on her hat.

MARIE-LOUISE. I see. Bentley told me she was upstairs. Goodbye. I shall only be a minute.

(BERNARD *goes into the adjoining room* R., *just as* JOHN *enters up* C.)

Oh John, I'm sorry to drag you away from your patients.

JOHN (*moving down*, R. *of* MARIE-LOUISE). There's nothing urgent. They can wait for a few minutes.

MARIE-LOUISE. Oh, John !

(BERNARD *has closed the door behind him and* JOHN'S *tone changes. They speak now in a low voice and quickly.*)

JOHN (*in a low voice*). Is anything the matter ?

MARIE-LOUISE (*nodding*). Mortimer.

JOHN. What about Mortimer ?

MARIE-LOUISE. I'm convinced he suspects.

JOHN. Suspects. Why ?

MARIE-LOUISE. He was so funny last night. He came into my room to say good night to me. He sat on my bed. He was chatting nicely and he was asking what I'd been doing with myself all the evening . . .

JOHN. Presumably you didn't tell him ?

MARIE-LOUISE. No, I said I'd been dining here. And suddenly he got up and just said good night and went out. His voice was so strange that I couldn't help looking at him. He was as red as a turkey-cock.

JOHN. Is that all ?

MARIE-LOUISE. No ! (*Crossing* JOHN *to below the sofa*.) He never came in to say good morning to me before he went to the City.

JOHN. He may have been in a hurry.

MARIE-LOUISE (*turning*). He's never in too much of a hurry for that.

JOHN. I think you're making a mountain of a mole-heap.

MARIE-LOUISE (*turning away*). Don't be stupid, John. (*Crossing down* R.) Can't you see I'm as nervous as a cat ?

JOHN (*down* C.). I can. But I'm trying to persuade you there's nothing to be nervous about.

MARIE-LOUISE (*turning to him*). What fools men are. (*Moving up* R. *of the sofa and then to* C.) They never will see that it's the small things that matter. I tell you I'm frightened out of my wits. (*She moves down* R.C.)

JOHN. You know there's a devil of a distance between suspicion and proof.

MARIE-LOUISE. Oh, I don't think he could prove anything. (*Moving to below the* R. *end of the sofa.*) But he can make himself awfully unpleasant. (*Turning.*) Supposing he put ideas in Constance's head ?

JOHN (*moving to* L. *of the sofa*). She'd never believe him.

MARIE-LOUISE. If the worst came to worst I could manage Mortimer. He's awfully in love with me. That always gives one such an advantage over a man.

JOHN (*going to her*). Of course you can twist Mortimer round your little finger.

MARIE-LOUISE. I should die of shame if Constance knew. After all, she's my greatest friend and I'm absolutely devoted to her.

JOHN. Constance is grand. (*Easing away* L.) Of course I don't believe there's anything in this at all, but if there were, I'd be in favour of making a clean breast of it to Constance.

MARIE-LOUISE. Never !

JOHN (*turning at* C.). I expect she'd kick up a row. Any woman would. But she'd do anything in the world to help us out.

MARIE-LOUISE. A lot you know about women. She'd help you out, I daresay. But she'd stamp on me with both feet. That's only human nature.

JOHN. Not Constance's.

MARIE-LOUISE (*moving towards* JOHN). Upon my word, it's lucky I'm fairly sure of you, John, or the way you talk of Constance would really make me jealous. (*She smiles a little.*)

JOHN. Thank God you can smile. Now you're getting your nerve back.

MARIE-LOUISE (*close to him*). It's been a comfort to talk it over. It doesn't seem so bad now.

JOHN. I'm sure you've got nothing to be frightened about.

MARIE-LOUISE. I daresay it was only my fancy. It was a stupid risk to take all the same.

JOHN. Perhaps. Why did you look so devilish pretty ?

MARIE-LOUISE. Oughtn't you to be getting back to your wretched patients ?

JOHN. I suppose so. Will you stop and see Constance ?

MARIE-LOUISE. I may as well. (*Crossing* JOHN *to down* L.) It would look rather odd if I went away without saying how d'you do to her.

JOHN (*moving up* C.). I'll leave you, then. (*Turning, below the door.*) And don't worry.

MARIE-LOUISE. I won't. I daresay it was only a guilty conscience. (*Easing up a little.*) I'll go and have my hair washed.

(*As* JOHN *turns to go out,* MARTHA *enters up* R., *followed by* BERNARD. MARTHA *moves to* R.C., *while* BERNARD *drops down* R. *of the sofa.*)

MARTHA (*with an almost exaggerated cordiality*). I had no idea you were here, Marie-Louise.

MARIE-LOUISE. It's not very important.

MARTHA. I was just writing letters, waiting for mother, and Bernard's only just told me.

MARIE-LOUISE. I wanted to see John about something.

MARTHA. I hope you haven't got anything the matter with you, darling.

MARIE-LOUISE. No. Mortimer's been looking rather run-down lately, and I want John to persuade him to take a holiday.

MARTHA. Oh, I should have thought he'd be more likely to take a physician's advice than a surgeon's in a thing like that.

MARIE-LOUISE. He's got a tremendous belief in John, you know.

MARTHA. In which I'm sure he's justified. John is so very reliable.

JOHN. What can I do for you, Martha ? If you'd like me to cut out an appendix or a few tonsils I shall be happy to oblige you.

MARTHA. My dear John, you've only left me the barest necessities of existence as it is. I don't think I could manage with anything less than I have.

JOHN. My dear, as long as a woman has a leg to stand on she need not despair of exciting her surgeon's sympathy and interest. (*He turns up,* R. *of the doors.*)

(CONSTANCE *enters up* C., *followed by* MRS. CULVER. CONSTANCE *moves down towards* MARIE-LOUISE.)

MARIE-LOUISE (*kissing her*). Darling.

CONSTANCE. How is your knee, still slipping ?

MARIE-LOUISE (*above the low table,* L.). It always gives me a little trouble, you know.

CONSTANCE (*crossing to the desk*). Yes, of course.

MRS. CULVER (*moving to* L. *of* MARTHA). I'm sorry I've been so long, Martha. Have you been very impatient ?

MARTHA (*easing to* R. *of the sofa*). No, I've been passing the time very pleasantly.

MRS. CULVER (*moving down,* L. *of the sofa*). For others, darling, or only for yourself ? (*She sits.*)

CONSTANCE (*at* L.C.). Bernard is taking me out to Wimbledon.

JOHN (*on her* R.). Oh, that'll be jolly. (*He eases to the* L. *end of the sofa.*)

BERNARD (*down* R.). We shall be dreadfully late.

CONSTANCE. Does it matter ? (*She sits on the piano stool.*)

BERNARD. No. (*He sits, down* R.)

(BENTLEY *enters up c., with a card on a small salver and takes it to*
        CONSTANCE. *She looks at the card and hesitates.*)

CONSTANCE. How very odd.
JOHN. What's the matter, Constance ?
CONSTANCE. Nothing. (*For an instant she reflects.*) Is he
downstairs ?
BENTLEY. Yes, madam.
CONSTANCE. I don't know why he should send up a card. Show
him up.
BENTLEY. Very good, madam.

(*Exit* BENTLEY.)

JOHN (*easing to c.*). Who is it, Constance ?
CONSTANCE. Come and sit down, Marie-Louise. (*She indicates
the piano stool on which she is sitting.*)
MARIE-LOUISE (*moving up* L.C.). I must go and so must you.
CONSTANCE. There's plenty of time. Do you like this hat ?
MARIE-LOUISE. Yes. I think it's sweet. (*She sits* L. *of* CONSTANCE.)
CONSTANCE. What are *you* doing here, John ? Haven't you got
any patients today ?
JOHN (L. *of the sofa*). Yes, there are two or three waiting. I'm
just going down. As a matter of fact I thought I deserved a cigarette.
(*He puts his hand to his hip pocket.*) Hang, I've mislaid my cigarette-
case. You haven't seen it about, Constance ?

(MARTHA *sits at the* R. *end of the sofa, facing* L.)

CONSTANCE. No, I haven't.
JOHN. I looked for it everywhere this morning. I can't think
where I left it. I must ring up the nursing-home and ask if I left it
there.
CONSTANCE. I hope you haven't lost it.
JOHN. Oh, no. I'm sure I haven't. I've just put it somewhere.

(*The doors up c. open and* BENTLEY *announces the visitor.*)

BENTLEY. Mr. Mortimer Durham.
MARIE-LOUISE (*startled out of her wits*). Oh !
CONSTANCE (*quickly, seizing her wrist*). Sit still !

(MORTIMER DURHAM *enters. He is a stoutish, biggish man of about
forty, with a red face and an irascible manner. At the moment
he is a prey to violent emotion. He moves down* c. *a few paces.*
BENTLEY *goes out.*)

(*Rising.*) Hulloa, Mortimer. What are you doing in these parts
at this hour ? Why on earth did you send up a card ?
MARIE-LOUISE. What's the matter, Morty ?

(MORTIMER *stops, up* c., *looks around, and then turns to* CONSTANCE.)

c

MORTIMER (*to* CONSTANCE, *with difficulty restraining his fury*). I thought you might like to know that your husband is my wife's lover.

MARIE-LOUISE (*rising*). Morty ! (*She breaks downstage and a little* L.)

CONSTANCE (*keeping a firm hand on* MARIE-LOUISE ; *very coolly to* MORTIMER). Oh ! What makes you think that ?

MORTIMER (*taking a gold cigarette-case out of his pocket*). Do you recognise this ? I found it under my wife's pillow last night.

CONSTANCE. Oh, I *am* relieved. I couldn't make out where I'd left it. (*Taking it from him.*) Thank you so much.

MORTIMER (*angrily*). It's not yours.

CONSTANCE. Indeed it is. I was sitting on Marie-Louise's bed and I must have slipped it under the pillow without thinking.

MORTIMER. It has John's initials on it.

CONSTANCE. I know. It was presented to him by a grateful patient, and I thought it much too nice for him, so I just took it.

MORTIMER. What sort of fool do you take me for, Constance ?

CONSTANCE. My dear Morty, why should I say it was my cigarette-case if it wasn't ?

MORTIMER. They had dinner together.

CONSTANCE. My poor Morty. I know that. You were going to a City banquet or something, and Marie-Louise rang up and asked if she might come and take pot-luck with us.

MORTIMER. Do you mean to say she dined here ?

CONSTANCE. Isn't that what she told you ?

MORTIMER. Yes.

CONSTANCE. It's quite easy to prove. If you won't take my word for it we can ring for the butler and you can ask him yourself . . . Ring the bell, John, will you ?

(JOHN *makes a move towards the bell-push.*)

MORTIMER (*uneasily*). No, don't do that.

(JOHN *checks.*)

If you give me your word, of course I must take it.

CONSTANCE. That's very kind of you. I'm grateful to you for not exposing me to the humiliation of making my butler corroborate my statement.

(JOHN *eases down* R.C. *a little.*)

MORTIMER. If Marie-Louise was dining here, why were you sitting on her bed ?

CONSTANCE. John had to go out and do an operation, and Marie-Louise wanted to show me the things she'd got from Paris, so I walked round to your house. It was a lovely night. You remember that, don't you ?

MORTIMER. Damn it, I've got more important things to do than look at the night.

CONSTANCE. We tried them all on and then we were rather tired, so Marie-Louise got into bed and I sat down and we talked.

MORTIMER. If you were tired why didn't you go home and go to bed ?

CONSTANCE. John had promised to come round and fetch me.

MORTIMER. And did he ? What time did he come ?

JOHN (by the L. end of the sofa). I couldn't manage it. The operation took much longer than I expected. It was one of those cases where when you once start cutting you really don't know where to stop. You know the sort of thing, don't you Mortimer ?

MORTIMER. No, I don't. How the devil should I ?

CONSTANCE. All that is neither here nor there. This is a terrible accusation you've made against John and Marie-Louise and I'm very much upset. But I will remain perfectly calm till I've heard everything. Now let me have your proofs.

MORTIMER. My proofs ? What d'you mean ? The cigarette-case. When I found the cigarette-case I naturally put two and two together.

CONSTANCE (with her eyes flashing). I quite understand, but why did you make them five ?

MORTIMER (emphatically, in order not to show that he is wavering). It isn't possible that I should have made a mistake.

CONSTANCE. Even the best of us may err.

MORTIMER (uneasily). You don't know what a shock it was, Constance. I had the most implicit confidence in Marie-Louise. I was knocked endways. I've been brooding over it ever since.

CONSTANCE (cutting in). And do you mean to say that you've come here and made a fearful scene just because you found my cigarette-case in Marie-Louise's room ? I can't believe it.

(MARIE-LOUISE gives a little sob and begins to weep, quietly, sitting down. L.)

You're a man of the world. You're extremely intelligent. Surely you have something to go upon. You must be holding something back. Don't be afraid of hurting my feelings. You've said so much now that I must insist on your saying everything. I want the truth and the whole truth.

(There is a pause. JOHN breaks R. above the sofa and turns. MORTIMER looks from MARIE-LOUISE, who is still weeping, to CONSTANCE, with the utmost bewilderment.)

MORTIMER (turning towards the sofa). I'm afraid I've made a damned fool of myself.

CONSTANCE. I'm afraid you have.

MORTIMER (turning back). I'm awfully sorry, Constance. I beg your pardon.

CONSTANCE. Oh, don't bother about me. You've exposed me to the most bitter humiliation. You've sown seeds of distrust between me and John which can never be . . . (*She searches for a word.*)

MRS. CULVER (*supplying one*). Fertilized.

CONSTANCE (*ignoring it*). Uprooted. But I don't matter. It's Marie-Louise's pardon you must beg.

(MARIE-LOUISE *rises and goes up* C., *towards the doors.*)

MORTIMER (*humbly*). Marie-Louise.

MARIE-LOUISE (L. *of* MORTIMER, *checking*). Don't touch me. Don't come near me. (*She passes him and eases to* R. *of the piano.*)

MORTIMER (*to* CONSTANCE, *miserably*). You know what jealousy is.

CONSTANCE. Certainly not. I think it's a most ugly and despicable vice. (*She eases away to* L. *of the low table.*)

MORTIMER (*to* MARIE-LOUISE). Marie-Louise, I'm sorry. Won't you forgive me ?

MARIE-LOUISE (*moving to below the piano stool*). You've insulted me before all my friends. You know how devotedly I love Constance. You might have accused me of having an affair with anyone else— but not John.

CONSTANCE. Not her greatest friend's husband. The milkman or the dustman if you like, but not her greatest friend's husband.

MORTIMER. I've been a perfect swine. I don't know what came over me. I really wasn't responsible for my actions.

MARIE-LOUISE. I've loved you all these years. No one has ever loved you as I've loved you. Oh, it's cruel, cruel !

MORTIMER (*taking a pace to her*). Come away, darling. I can't say here what I want to say.

MARIE-LOUISE (*turning away*). No, no, no ! (*She goes to* L. *of the piano and leans over it weeping.*)

CONSTANCE (*crossing to* L. *of* MORTIMER *and putting her hand on his arm gently*). I think you'd better leave her here for a little while, Morty. I'll talk to her when you've gone. She's naturally upset. A sensitive little thing like that.

(MARIE-LOUISE *moves from the piano to the desk chair, facing* L.)

MORTIMER. We're dining with the Vancouvers.

CONSTANCE (*taking* MORTIMER *up* C. *towards the door*). I promise I'll send her home in good time to dress.

MORTIMER. She'll give me another chance ?

CONSTANCE. Yes, yes.

MORTIMER. I'd do anything in the world for her.

(CONSTANCE *puts her fingers to her lips and then points significantly to the pearl chain she is wearing. For a second* MORTIMER *does not understand, but as soon as her notion dawns on him he gives a pleased nod.*)

You're the cleverest woman in the world. (*As he goes out he stops, turns, and holds out his hand to* JOHN.) Will you shake hands with me, old man ? I made a mistake and I'm man enough to acknowledge it.

JOHN (*very cordially*). Not at all, old boy. I quite agree that it did look fishy—the cigarette-case. If I'd dreamt that Constance was going to leave an expensive thing like that lying about all over the place, I'm hanged if I'd have let her pinch it.

MORTIMER. You don't know what a weight it is off my mind. I felt a hundred when I came here, and now I feel like a two-year-old.

(*He turns and exits. The moment the door is closed behind him there is a general change in every attitude. The tension disappears and there is a feeling of relief.*)

JOHN (*at* C.). Constance, you're a brick. I shall never forget this. Never, so long as I live. And by George, what presence of mind you showed. I went hot and cold all over, and you never batted an eyelash.

CONSTANCE. By the way, here is your cigarette-case. You'd better have a ring made and hang it on your key-chain.

JOHN (*taking it, after a slight hesitation*). Thank you.

CONSTANCE. By the way, did anyone see you go into Morty's house last night ?

JOHN. No, we let ourselves in with Marie-Louise's latch-key.

CONSTANCE. That's all right then. If Mortimer asks the servants they can tell him nothing. I had to take that chance. (*She eases away* L.)

MARIE-LOUISE (*facing* CONSTANCE, *with a little gesture of ashamed dismay*). Oh, Constance, what must you think of me ?

CONSTANCE. I ? Exactly the same as I thought before. (*Sitting on the piano stool.*) I think you're sweet, Marie-Louise.

MARIE-LOUISE. You have every right to be angry with me.

CONSTANCE. Perhaps, but not the inclination.

MARIE-LOUISE (*moving below and* L. *of the piano*). You had your chance to get back on me and you didn't take it. I'm so ashamed.

CONSTANCE (*amused*). Because you've been having an affair with John, or because you've been found out ?

MARIE-LOUISE (*moving down to the chair* L.). Oh, Constance, don't be heartless. Say anything you like, curse me, stamp on me, but don't smile at me. I'm in a terrible position.

CONSTANCE. And you want me to make a scene. I know and I sympathise. (*Very calmly.*) But the fact is that Mortimer told me nothing I didn't know before.

MARIE-LOUISE (*turning ; aghast*). Do you mean to say that you've known all along ?

CONSTANCE. All along, darling. I've been spending the last six months in a desperate effort to prevent my friends and relations from telling me your ghastly secret. It's been very difficult sometimes. Often mother's profound understanding of life, Martha's passion for truth at any price, and Barbara's silent sympathy, have almost worn me down. (*She rises.*) But until today the t's were not definitely crossed nor the i's distinctly dotted, and I was able to ignore the facts that were staring at me—rather rudely, I must say—in the face.

MARIE-LOUISE. But why, why ? It's not human. Why didn't you do anything ?

CONSTANCE (*easing down, above and* R. *of* MARIE-LOUISE). That, darling, is my affair.

MARIE-LOUISE (*thinking she understands*). Oh, I see.

CONSTANCE (*rather tartly*). No, you don't. I have always been absolutely faithful to John. I have not winked at your intrigue in order to cover my own.

MARIE-LOUISE (*beginning to be a little put out*). I almost think you've been laughing at me up your sleeve all the time.

CONSTANCE (*good-humouredly*). My dear, you mustn't be offended just because I've taken away from you the satisfaction of thinking that you have been deceiving me all these months. (*She moves* L. *to the desk, and looks out of the window.*)

MARIE-LOUISE (*rising and moving* C.). My head's going round and round.

CONSTANCE (*turning*). Such a pretty head, too. Why don't you go and lie down ? You want to look your best if you're dining with the Vancouvers.

MARIE-LOUISE (*below and* R. *of the piano*). I wonder where Mortimer is ?

CONSTANCE (*moving in a little*). You know that pearl necklace you showed me the other day and you said that Mortimer thought it cost a lot of money—well, he's going to Cartier's to buy it for you, tomorrow.

MARIE-LOUISE. Oh, Constance, do you think he will ?

CONSTANCE. Yes. But, my dear, don't be such a fool as to accept it with alacrity. Remember that Mortimer has grievously insulted you, he's made the most shocking accusation that a man can make against his wife, he's trampled on your love and now he's destroyed your trust in him.

MARIE-LOUISE. How right you are, Constance.

CONSTANCE. Surely I need not tell you what to do. Refuse to speak to him, but never let him get a word in edgeways. Cry enough to make him feel what a brute he is, but not enough to make your eyes red. Say the same thing over and over again, and when you've reduced him to desperation, then consent, as a sign of your forgiving nature, to accept the pearl necklace, for which the wretch has paid ten thousand pounds . . .

(*As* MARIE-LOUISE *is about to speak.*)

. . . and don't thank him. Let him thank you for accepting such a paltry gift. (*Turning to* JOHN.) John, take Marie-Louise down and put her in a taxi.

JOHN (*moving up*). All right.

MARIE-LOUISE.   No, not John. I couldn't. After all, I have some delicacy.

CONSTANCE.   Oh, have you ? Well, let Bernard go.

BERNARD (*rising*). I shall be pleased. (*He crosses above the sofa to the doors up* C.)

CONSTANCE (*to* BERNARD). But come back, won't you ?

BERNARD.   Certainly.

MARIE-LOUISE (*kissing* CONSTANCE). This has been a lesson to me, darling. I'm not a fool, Constance. I can learn.

CONSTANCE.   At least prudence, I hope.

(MARIE-LOUISE *exits, followed by* BERNARD.)

JOHN (*moving down to above and* L. *of the sofa*). How did you guess that Marie-Louise had said she was dining here ?

CONSTANCE (*at* L.C.). She's too crafty a woman to invent a new lie when an old one will do.

JOHN.   It would have been awkward if Mortimer had insisted on asking Bentley if it was true.

CONSTANCE.   I knew he wouldn't dare. It's only if a man's a gentleman that he won't hesitate to do an ungentlemanly thing. Mortimer is on the boundary line and it makes him careful.

MARTHA (*rising and easing* R., *significantly*). Don't you imagine your patients are growing a trifle restless, John ? (*She turns, down* R., *to face* JOHN.)

JOHN.   I like to keep them waiting.

MARTHA (*pursing her lips*). I can't imagine you'll very much like to hear what I'm determined to say to Constance.

JOHN.   It's because I shrewdly suspect that you have some very unpleasant things to say about me that I am prepared reluctantly to neglect the call of duty and listen to you with my own ears.

CONSTANCE (*crossing* R. *below the sofa*). She's been exercising miracles of restraint for the last three months, John. I think she has a right to let herself go now. (*She sits,* R. *of* MRS. CULVER.)

JOHN.   If she's suffering from suppressed desires she's come to the wrong establishment. She wants a psychoanalyst.

MARTHA (*moving across to* L., *below the sofa*). I've only got one thing to say, John, and I'm perfectly willing that you should hear it. (*At* L.C., *turning to* CONSTANCE.) I don't know what your reasons were for shielding that abominable woman. I can only suppose you wanted to avoid more scandal than was necessary . . .

MRS. CULVER (*interrupting*). Before you go any further, my dear, you must let me put my word in. (*To* CONSTANCE.) My dear child, I beg you not to decide anything in a hurry. We must all think things over. First of all you must listen to what John has to say for himself.

MARTHA (*turning up to the* R. *end of the piano stool*). What can he have to say for himself ?

CONSTANCE (*ironically*). What indeed ?

JOHN. Not the right thing, anyway. (*Moving down* L. *to the easy chair.*) I'm for it, and I'm prepared to take what's coming to me.

CONSTANCE (*to the world in general*). No man could say handsomer than that. (*She rises, eases a little* R., *and turns.*)

JOHN. I'm expecting you to make a scene, Constance. It's your right and your privilege. I'm willing to bear it. Give me hell. I deserve it. My name is mud.

CONSTANCE (*moving below the sofa to* R.C.). My poor John, what is there to make a scene about ?

JOHN. I know how badly I've treated you. I had a wife who was good, loving and faithful, devoted to my interests, a perfect mother and an excellent housekeeper ; a woman ten times too good for me. If I'd had the smallest spark of decency I couldn't have treated you like this. I haven't a word to say for myself.

MARTHA (*interrupting him*). You've humiliated her to all her friends.

JOHN. I've behaved neither like a gentleman nor a sportsman.

MARTHA. Your conduct is inexcusable.

JOHN. I haven't a leg to stand on.

MARTHA. Even if you didn't love her, you might have treated her with respect.

JOHN. I've been as heartless as a crocodile and as unscrupulous as a typhoid bacillus.

CONSTANCE (*crossing to the piano stool*). Between you, of course, you're leaving me very little to say. (*She sits.*)

MARTHA. There is nothing to say. You're quite right. This is the sort of occasion when it's beneath a woman's dignity to make a scene. (*To* JOHN, *moving down* L.C.) I suppose you'll have the decency to put no obstacle in the way of Constance's getting her freedom ?

MRS. CULVER. Oh, Constance, you're not going to divorce him ?

MARTHA (*crossing below the sofa to down* R.). Mother, you're so weak. How can she go on living with a man for whom she has no respect ?

CONSTANCE. John has always been an excellent father. Let us give the devil his due.

MRS. CULVER (*rising*). Don't be too hard, darling. (*She moves across to* R. *of* CONSTANCE.) I can understand that at the moment you feel bitter, but it would be very sad if you let your bitterness warp your judgment.

CONSTANCE. I don't feel in the least bitter. I wish I looked as sweet as I feel.

MRS. CULVER. Of course John is to blame. I admit that. He's been very, very naughty. But men are weak and women are so unscrupulous. I'm sure he's sorry for all the pain he's caused you.

MARTHA (*below and* R. *of the sofa*). What puzzles me is that you didn't do something the moment you discovered that John was having an affair.

CONSTANCE. To tell you the truth, I thought it no business of mine.

MARTHA (*indignantly*). Aren't you his wife ?

CONSTANCE (*rising*). John and I are very lucky people. (*Moving towards the sofa.*) Our marriage has been ideal.

MARTHA. How can you say that ?

CONSTANCE (*at* C.). For five years we adored each other. That's much longer than most people do. Our honeymoon lasted five years and then we had a most extraordinary stroke of luck ; we ceased to be in love with one another simultaneously.

JOHN (*sitting erect*). I protest, Constance. I've never ceased to be absolutely devoted to you.

(MRS. CULVER *sits on the piano stool.*)

CONSTANCE (*facing* JOHN). I never said you had, darling. I'm convinced of it. I've never ceased to be devoted to you. We've shared one another's interests, we've loved to be together, we've laughed at the same jokes and sighed over the same worries. I don't know any couple that's been bound together by a more genuine affection. But honestly, for the last ten years have you been in love with me ?

JOHN (*sitting back*). You can't expect a man who's been married for fifteen years . . .

CONSTANCE. My dear, I'm not asking for excuses. I'm only asking for a plain answer.

JOHN. In the long run I enjoy your society much more than anybody else's. There's no one I like so much as you. You're the prettiest woman I've ever known and I shall say the same when you're a hundred.

CONSTANCE. But does your heart leap into your mouth when you hear my footstep on the stairs, and when I come into the room is your first impulse to catch me in your manly arms ? I haven't noticed it.

JOHN. I don't want to make a fool of myself.

CONSTANCE. Then I think you've answered my question. You're no more in love with me than I am with you.

JOHN. You never said a word of this before.

CONSTANCE. I think most married couples tell each other too much.

JOHN. How did you find out ?

CONSTANCE. I'll tell you. One night as we were dancing together, all at once I noticed that we weren't keeping such good step as we generally did. It was because my mind was wandering. I was thinking how it would suit me to do my hair like a woman who was dancing alongside of us. Then I looked at you and I saw you were thinking what pretty legs she'd got. I suddenly realised that you weren't in love with me any more and at the same moment I realised that it was a relief, because I wasn't in love with you.

JOHN. I must say it never occurred to me for a moment.

CONSTANCE. I know. A man thinks it quite natural that he should fall out of love with a woman, but it never strikes him for a moment that a woman can do anything so unnatural as to fall out of love with him. Don't be upset at that, darling; that is one of the charming limitations of your sex.

MARTHA (*taking a pace below the sofa*). Do you mean mother and me to understand that sin.e then John has been having one affair after another and you haven't turned a hair ?

CONSTANCE. Since this is the first time he's been found out, let us give him the benefit of the doubt. You're not angry with me, John ?

JOHN. No, darling, not angry. But I *am* a little taken aback. I think you've been making rather a damned fool of me. It never struck me that your feelings for me had changed so much. You can't expect me to like it.

CONSTANCE (*moving down* L., *above and to* R. *of* JOHN). Oh, come now, you must be reasonable. You surely wouldn't wish me to have languished for all these years in a hopeless passion for you when you had nothing to give me in return but friendship and affection. Think what a bore it is to have someone in love with you whom you're not in love with.

JOHN. I can't conceive of your ever being a bore, Constance.

CONSTANCE. Don't you realise that we must thank our lucky stars ? We are the favoured of the Gods. I shall never forget those five years of exquisite happiness you gave me when I loved you, and I shall never cease to be grateful for them. Not because you loved me, but because you inspired me with love. (*Breaking* R. *to* C.) Our love was like a cross-word puzzle in which we both hit upon the last word at the same moment. (*Turning to face* JOHN.) That is why our lives have been so happy. That is why ours is a perfect marriage.

MARTHA. Do you mean to say that it meant nothing to you when you found out that John was carrying on with Marie-Louise ?

CONSTANCE (*turning to* MARTHA). Human nature is very imperfect; I am afraid I must admit that at the first moment I was vexed, but only at the first moment. Then I reflected that it was unreasonable to be angry with John for giving to another something I had no use for. That would be too much like a dog in the manger, and then I was fond enough of John to be willing that he should be happy in his own way, and if he is going to indulge in an intrigue . . . isn't that the proper phrase, John ?

JOHN. I have not yet made up my mind whether it really is an indulgence.

CONSTANCE. Then it was much better that the object of his affection should be so intimate a friend of mine that I could keep a maternal eye on him.

JOHN. Really, Constance.

CONSTANCE. Marie-Louise is not clever enough to acquire any ascendancy over him and so long as I kept his heart I was quite willing that she should have his senses. If you wanted to deceive me, John, I couldn't have chosen anyone with whom I would more willingly be deceived than Marie-Louise.

JOHN (*rising and crossing* C. *to* L. *of* CONSTANCE). I don't gather that you have been very grossly deceived, darling. You have such penetration that when you look at me I feel as though I were shivering without a stitch of clothing on. (*He eases away to* R. *of the piano.*)

MRS. CULVER (*rising*). I don't approve of your a titude, Constance. (*Crossing down* L. *and turning, to them.*) In my day when a young wife discovered that her husband had been deceiving her, she burst into a flood of tears and went to stay with her mother for three weeks, not returning to her husband till he had been brought to a proper state of abjection and repentance.

MARTHA. Are we to understand then that you are not going to divorce John ?

CONSTANCE. You know, I can never see why a woman should give up a comfortable home, a considerable part of her income and the advantage of having a man about, because he has been unfaithful to her. She's merely cutting off her nose to spite her face.

(MRS. CULVER *sits down* L.)

MARTHA. I am at a loss for words.

CONSTANCE (*turning to* JOHN). You've been very stupid, my poor John.

JOHN. I've been a fool, Constance. (*To below the piano stool.*) I know it, but I'm capable of learning by experience, so I can't be a damned fool. (*He sits.*)

CONSTANCE. You mean that in the future you'll be more careful to cover your tracks ?

MRS. CULVER. Oh no, Constance, he means that this has been a lesson to him, and that in the future you'll have no cause for complaint.

JOHN. Constance, I give you my word of honour . . .

CONSTANCE (*interrupting*). That is the only gift you can make for which I can find no use. You see, so long as I was able to pretend a blissful ignorance of your goings-on we could all be perfectly happy. You were enjoying yourself, and I received a lot of sympathy as the outraged wife. But now I do see that the position is very difficult. You have put me in a position that is neither elegant nor dignified.

JOHN. I'm awfully sorry, Constance.

MARTHA. You're going to leave him ?

CONSTANCE. No, I'm not going to leave him. (*She sits on the* L. *arm of the sofa.*) John, you remember that Barbara offered to take me into her business ? I refused. Well, I've changed my mind, and I'm going to accept.

JOHN. But why ? I don't see your point.

CONSTANCE. I'm not prepared any more to be entirely dependent upon you.

JOHN. But my dear, everything I earn is at your disposal. It's a pleasure for me to provide for your wants. Heaven knows they are not very great.

CONSTANCE. I know. Come, John, I've been reasonable, haven't I ? Don't try and thwart me, when I want to do something on which I have set my heart.

JOHN (*rising*). I don't understand but if you put it like that I haven't a word to say. (*Moving to* C.) Of course, you must do exactly as you wish.

CONSTANCE (*rising*). That's a dear. Oughtn't you to go back to your patients ? Or else I shall have to keep you as well as myself.

JOHN (*crossing to* CONSTANCE). Will you give me a kiss before I go ?

CONSTANCE. Why not ?

JOHN (*kissing her*). It's peace between us ?

CONSTANCE. Peace and goodwill.

(JOHN *exits up* C.)

He is rather sweet, isn't he ?

MARTHA. Not in *my* opinion.

MRS. CULVER. What have you got in your mind, Constance ?.

CONSTANCE (*moving a little down* L.C.). I, mother ? (*Teasing her.*) What do you suspect ?

MRS. CULVER. I don't like the look of you.

CONSTANCE. I'm sorry for that. Most people find me far from plain.

MRS. CULVER. You've some devilry in mind. But for the life of me I can't guess it.

MARTHA. I can't see what you expect to get out of working for Barbara.

CONSTANCE. Between a thousand and fifteen hundred a year, I believe.

MARTHA. I wasn't thinking of the money, and you know it.

CONSTANCE. I am tired of being the modern wife.

MARTHA. What do you mean by the modern wife ?

CONSTANCE. A prostitute who doesn't deliver the goods.

MRS. CULVER. My dear, what would your father say if he heard you say such things ?

CONSTANCE. Darling, need we conjecture the remarks of a gentleman who's been dead for five and twenty years ? Had he any gift for repartee ?

MRS. CULVER. None whatever. He was good, but he was stupid. That is why the gods loved him and he died young.

(BERNARD *opens the door and looks in.*)

BERNARD. May I come in ?

CONSTANCE (*turning*). Oh, there you are. I wondered what had become of you. (*Turning to* MRS. CULVER.) Well, mother, I won't detain you any longer. I know that you and Martha have a thousand things to do.

MRS. CULVER (*rising*). I'm glad you reminded me. Come, Martha. Good-bye darling. (*Moving up* C.) Good-bye, Mr. Kersal.

BERNARD. Good-bye.

(MRS. CULVER *moves up to the doors* C.   MARTHA *crosses below the sofa to* C.)

CONSTANCE (*to* MARTHA). Good-bye, dear. Thank you for all your sympathy. You've been a great help in my hour of need.

MARTHA. I don't understand and it's no good saying I do.

CONSTANCE. Bless you.

(MARTHA *turns, goes up* C., *and exits with* MRS. CULVER. BERNARD *closes the door after them.*)

(*Moving up to the piano stool.*) Shall we be very late ?

BERNARD (*moving down* C.). So late that it doesn't matter if we're a little later. I have something important to say to you.

CONSTANCE (*teasing him a little*). Important to me or important to you ?

BERNARD. I can't tell you how distressed I was at that terrible scene.

CONSTANCE (*crossing below* BERNARD *to* R. *of the sofa*). Oh, didn't you think it had its lighter moments ?

BERNARD (*moving to* L. *of the sofa*). It's only this afternoon I learned the truth, and then I never imagined for a moment that you knew it too. I can't tell you how brave I think it of you . . .

CONSTANCE (*cutting in*). You're very sweet, Bernard. (*She sits at the* R. *end of the sofa, facing him.*)

BERNARD (*moving above the sofa,* L. *of* CONSTANCE). When I think of what you've gone through . . .

CONSTANCE (*with a quick smile*). It's not a very good plan to take other people's misfortunes too much to heart.

BERNARD (*leaning slightly over the back of the sofa*). You know that if things were as I thought they were between you and John nothing would have induced me to say a word. But now he has no longer any claims on you. He doesn't love you. Why should you go on wasting your life with a man who is capable of exposing you to all this humiliation ? You know how long and tenderly I have loved you. You can trust yourself to me. I'll give my whole life to making you forget the anguish you've endured. (*Bending towards her.*) Will you marry me, Constance ?

CONSTANCE. My dear, John may have behaved very badly, but he's still my husband.

BERNARD (*straightening up*). Only in name. You've done everything in your power to save a scandal and now if you ask him to let himself be divorced he's bound to consent.

CONSTANCE. Do you really think John has behaved so very badly to me ?

BERNARD (*astonished*). You don't mean to say that you have any doubts in your mind as to his relationship with Marie-Louise ?

CONSTANCE. None.

BERNARD. Then what in God's name do you mean ?

CONSTANCE. My dear Bernard, have you ever considered what marriage is among well-to-do people ? The house is managed by servants ; nurses look after her children, if she's resigned herself to having any ; and as soon as they are old enough she packs them off to school. Let us face it, she is no more than the mistress of the man whose desire she has taken advantage of to insist on a legal ceremony that will prevent him from discarding her when his desire has ceased.

BERNARD. I don't agree with you. (*Moving away*, C.) She's also his companion and helpmate.

CONSTANCE. You see, my poor friend, you are in love and your judgment is confused.

BERNARD (*turning at* C.). I don't understand what you mean.

CONSTANCE. John gives me board and lodgings, money for my clothes and my amusements, a car, and a certain position in the world. He's bound to do all that, because fifteen years ago, he was madly in love with me and he undertook it. Don't you think it would be very shabby of me to take advantage now of his generosity or his want of foresight ?

BERNARD. In what way ?

CONSTANCE. He paid a very high price for something that he couldn't get cheaper. He no longer wants that. Why should I resent it ? I know as well as anybody else that desire is fleeting. It comes and goes and no man can understand why. The only thing that's certain is that when it's gone it's gone for ever.

BERNARD (*moving to the* L. *end of the sofa*). That might be all right if a man had only to think about himself ? What about the woman ?

CONSTANCE. I don't think you need waste too much sympathy on her. (*Thoughtfully, not looking at* BERNARD.) When the average woman has been married for fifteen years and discovers her husband's infidelity, it is not her heart that is wounded, but her vanity. If she had any sense she would regard it merely as one of the necessary inconveniences of an otherwise pleasant profession.

BERNARD (*after a slight pause*). The long and short of it is that you don't love me.

CONSTANCE (*looking up at* BERNARD, *smiling*). You think that my principles are all moonshine ?

BERNARD (*moving away* L.). I don't think they would have much influence if you were as crazy about me as I am about you. (*Turning at* L.C.) Do you still love John ?

CONSTANCE (*rising*). I am very fond of him. (*Moving slowly across to* R. *of* BERNARD.) He makes me laugh, and we get on together like a house on fire, but I'm not in love with him.

BERNARD.   And is that enough for you ? Isn't the future some-times a trifle desolate ? Don't you want love ?

(*A pause.* CONSTANCE *gives him a long reflective look.*)

CONSTANCE.   If I did I should come to you for it, Bernard.

BERNARD.   Constance.   (*He seizes her in his arms and kisses her passionately.*)

CONSTANCE (*releasing herself*).   Oh, my dear, don't be so sudden.

BERNARD.   But if you love me ?

CONSTANCE.   I never said I did.   (*Crossing below him, down* L.) But even if I did, so long as John provides me with all the necessities of existence I wouldn't be unfaithful.   (*Turning.*) It all comes down to the economic situation.

BERNARD.   Do you mean to say there's no hope at all ?

CONSTANCE.   The only hope before you at the moment is to start for Wimbledon before the game is over.

BERNARD.   Do you still want to go ?

CONSTANCE.   Yes.

BERNARD.   Very well.   (*He pauses.*) But—I love you.

CONSTANCE.   Then go down and start up the car, and I'll join you in a minute; I want to phone.   (*She goes* L. *to the low table.*)

BERNARD (*going up* C.).   Very well.

(*He exits.* CONSTANCE *dials a number.*)

CONSTANCE.   Barbara ? It's Constance. That offer you made me a fortnight ago, is it still open ? Well, I want to accept it . . . No, no. Nothing has happened. John is very well. He's always sweet, you know. It's only that I want to earn my own living. When can I start ? . . .   The sooner the better.

CURTAIN.

ACT III

SCENE: The same.   One year later.   Afternoon.

When the CURTAIN *rises* CONSTANCE *is seated* L. *at the desk, writing letters.* BENTLEY *enters up* C., *and shows in* BARBARA FAWCETT *and* MARTHA.

BENTLEY.   Mrs. Fawcett, and Miss Culver.

(BENTLEY *exits.*)

CONSTANCE (*turning in her chair*).   Oh !   Sit down.   I'm just finishing a note.   (*She goes on writing.*)

BARBARA (*moving to* L.C.).   We met on the doorstep.

MARTHA (*moving down and below the sofa,* R.).   I thought I'd just look round and see if there was anything I could do to help you before you start.

CONSTANCE (*turning again, and looking across at* MARTHA). That's very nice of you, Martha.   I really don't think there is. (*Writing an envelope.*)   I'm packed and ready, and for once I don't believe I've forgotten one of the things I shan't want.   (*She puts the letter into the evelope.*)

BARBARA.   I felt I must run in to say good-bye to you.

CONSTANCE (*rising*).   Now, my dear, you musn't neglect your work the moment my back is turned.   (*She picks up a box of chocolates and brings it to* BARBARA, *offering them to her.*)

BARBARA (*taking a chocolate and eating it*).   Well, it's partly the work that's brought me.   An order has just come in for a new house and they want an Italian room.

CONSTANCE (*crossing to* MARTHA *with the chocolates*).   I don't like the look in your beady eye, Barbara.   (*She offers the chocolates to* MARTHA, *who takes one.*)

BARBARA (*moving down* L.).   Well, it struck me that as you're going to Italy you might go round the shops and buy any nice pieces that you can find.   (*She turns by the chair down* L.)

CONSTANCE (*returning to* C.).   Perish the thought.   I've worked like a dog for a year, and last night at six o'clock I downed tools. You said I could take six weeks' holiday.

BARBARA.   I admit that you've thoroughly earned it.

CONSTANCE (*moving up* C., *and putting the chocolates on the piano*).   I've worked hard and I've enjoyed my work, and now I'm going to enjoy a perfect holiday.

BARBARA.   Oh, well, have it your own way.   (*She sits on the chair* L.)

CONSTANCE (*moving from* R. *of the piano to below it*).   Yes, dear.

MARTHA.   Constance, dear, I think there's something you ought to know.

48

CONSTANCE (*turning at* L.C.). I should have thought you had discovered by now that I generally know the things I ought to know. (*She crosses* L. *to the desk*.)

MARTHA. You'll never guess whom I saw in Bond Street this morning.

CONSTANCE (*putting a stamp on her letter*). Yes, I shall. Marie-Louise. (*She puts the letter on the desk*.)

MARTHA. Oh !

CONSTANCE (*moving in, to* L.C.). I'm sorry to disappoint you, darling. She rang me up an hour ago.

MARTHA. But I thought she wasn't coming back for another month. She was going to stay away a year.

CONSTANCE (*moving to the* L. *end of the sofa*). She arrived last night and I'm expecting her every minute.

MARTHA. Here ?

CONSTANCE. Yes. She said she simply must run in and see me before I left.

MARTHA. I wonder what she wants.

CONSTANCE (*sitting on the* L. *arm of the sofa*). Perhaps to pass the time of day. I think it's rather sweet of her, considering how busy she must be on getting back after so long.

BARBARA. She's been all over the place, hasn't she ?

CONSTANCE. Yes, she's been in Malaya ; Mortimer has interests there, you know, and in China, and now they've just come from India.

MARTHA. I often wondered if it was at your suggestion that they set off on that long tour immediately after that unfortunate scene.

CONSTANCE. Which, you must confess, no one enjoyed more than you, darling.

BARBARA. It was certainly the most sensible thing they could do.

MARTHA. Of course you know your own business best, darling, but don't you think it's a little unfortunate that you should be going away for six weeks just as she comes back ?

CONSTANCE. We working women have to take our holidays when we can.

BARBARA. Surely John has had his lesson. He's not going to make a fool of himself a second time.

MARTHA. Do you think he has really got over his infatuation, Constance ?

CONSTANCE. I don't know at all.

(*The doors up* C. *open and* JOHN *enters*.)

But here he is, you'd better ask him.

JOHN (*moving down*). Ask him what ?

MARTHA (*not at all at a loss*). I was just wondering what you'd do with yourself during Constance's absence.

JOHN (*at* C.). I've got a lot of work, you know, and I shall be at the club a good deal. (*He crosses* L. *to the desk and busies himself*.)

MARTHA. It seems a pity that you weren't able to arrange things so that you and Constance could take your holidays together.

BARBARA. Don't blame me for that. I was quite willing to make my arrangements to suit Constance.

CONSTANCE. You see, I wanted to go to Italy and the only places John likes on the Continent are those in which it's only by an effort of the imagination that you can tell you're not in England.

MARTHA. What about Helen ?

CONSTANCE. We've taken a house at Henley for August. John can play golf and go on the river and I shall be able to come up to town every day to look after the business.

BARBARA (*rising*). Well, dear, I'll leave you. (*Moving up* C.) I hope you'll have a wonderful holiday. I know you've deserved it. (*Turning to face* JOHN.) Do you know, I think I'm a very clever woman, John, to have persuaded Constance to work. She's been absolutely invaluable to me.

JOHN (*who has moved in, to* L.C.). I never liked the idea and I'm not going to say I did.

BARBARA. Haven't you forgiven me yet ?

JOHN. She insisted on it and I had to make the best of a bad job.

BARBARA (*to* CONSTANCE). Good-bye.

CONSTANCE (*taking* BARBARA'S *hands*). Good-bye, dear. Take care of yourself. (*They kiss.*)

MARTHA (*rising*). I'll come with you, Barbara. (*She moves up* C.) Mother said she'd look in for a minute to say good-bye to you.

CONSTANCE. Oh, all right. Good-bye.

(*She kisses* MARTHA *and accompanies them to the door.* BARBARA *and* MARTHA *exit.* CONSTANCE *closes the doors and comes down.*)

JOHN (*moving across* R., *below the sofa*). I say, Constance, I thought you had to go now because Barbara couldn't possibly get away.

CONSTANCE (R. *of the piano*). Did I say that ?

JOHN. Certainly !

CONSTANCE (*picking up her handbag*). Oh !

JOHN (*turning,* R. *of the sofa*). If I'd dreamt that you could just as easily take your holiday when I take mine . . .

CONSTANCE (*interrupting, as she crosses to below the sofa*). Don't you think it's a mistake for husbands and wives to take their holidays together ? (*Sitting at the* L. *end of the sofa.*) The only reason one takes a holiday is for rest and change and recreation. Do you think a man really gets that when he goes away with his wife ?

JOHN. It depends on the wife.

CONSTANCE. I know nothing more depressing than the sight of all those couples in a hotel dining room, one little couple to one little table, sitting opposite to one another without a word to say.

JOHN. Oh, nonsense. You often see couples who are very jolly and cheerful.

CONSTANCE. Yes, I know, but look closely at the lady's wedding-ring, and you'll see that it rests uneasily on the hand it adorns. Anyhow, it's too late now. My bags are packed, my farewells made and nothing bores people so much as to see you tomorrow when they've made up their minds to get on without you for a month.

JOHN. H'm. Eyewash . . . (*A slight pause—he sits on the* R. *arm of the sofa.*) Look here, Constance, there's something I want to say to you.

CONSTANCE. Yes ?

JOHN. Do you know that Marie-Louise has come back ?

CONSTANCE. Yes. She said she'd try and look in to say how do you do before I started. It'll be nice to see her again after so long.

JOHN. I want you to do something for me, Constance. (*He sits on the sofa,* R. *of* CONSTANCE.)

CONSTANCE. What is it ?

JOHN. I haven't seen Marie-Louise since that day when Mortimer came here and made such a fool of himself. · She's been away for nearly a year and taking all things into consideration I think it would be a mistake to resume the relations that we were on then.

CONSTANCE. What makes you think she wishes to ?

JOHN. The fact that she rang you up the moment she arrived looks ominous to me.

CONSTANCE. Ominous ? You know some women can't see a telephone without taking the receiver off and then, when the operator says " Number, please," they have to say something. I daresay ours was the first that occurred to Marie-Louise.

JOHN. It's no good blinking the fact that Marie-Louise was madly in love with me.

CONSTANCE. Well, we can neither of us blame her for that.

JOHN. I don't want to be unkind, but after all, circumstances have forced a break upon us and I think we had better look upon it as permanent.

CONSTANCE. Of course you must please yourself.

JOHN. I'm not thinking of myself, Constance. I'm thinking partly of Marie-Louise's good, but, I confess chiefly of you. I could never look you in the face again if everything between Marie-Louise and me were not definitely finished.

CONSTANCE. I should hate you to lose so harmless and inexpensive a pleasure.

JOHN. Of course it'll be painful, but if one's made up one's mind to do a thing I think it's much better to do it quickly.

CONSTANCE. I think you're quite right. I'll tell you what I'll do, as soon as Marie-Louise comes I'll make an excuse and leave you alone with her.

JOHN (*rising and easing away* R.). That wasn't exactly my idea.

CONSTANCE. Oh ?

JOHN (*turning*). It's the kind of thing that a woman can do so much better than a man. It struck me that it would come better from you than from me.

CONSTANCE. Oh, did it?

JOHN. It's a little awkward for me, but it would be quite easy for you to say—well, you have your self-respect to think of, and to cut a long story short, she must either give me up or you'll raise hell.

CONSTANCE. But you know what a soft heart I have. If she bursts into tears and says she can't live without you I shall feel so sorry for her that I shall say, " Well, damn it all, keep him."

JOHN (*taking a quick pace to below the sofa*). You wouldn't do me a dirty trick like that, Constance.

CONSTANCE. You know that your happiness is my chief interest in life.

JOHN (*after a moment's hesitation, sitting* R. *of* CONSTANCE). Constance, I will be perfectly frank with you. I'm fed up with Marie-Louise.

CONSTANCE. Darling, why didn't you say that at once?

JOHN. Be a sport, Constance. You know that's not the kind of thing one can say to a woman.

CONSTANCE. I admit it's not the kind of thing she's apt to take very well.

JOHN. Women are funny. When they're tired of you they tell you so without a moment's hesitation and if you don't like it you can lump it. But if you're tired of them you're a brute and a beast and boiling oil's too good for you.

CONSTANCE (*patting his knee*). Very well, leave it to me. I'll do it.

JOHN (*kissing her*). You're a perfect brick. But you'll let her down gently, won't you? I wouldn't hurt her feelings for the world. (*Rising and moving towards* C.) She's a nice little thing, Constance.

CONSTANCE. Sweet.

JOHN. And it's hard luck on her.

CONSTANCE. Rotten.

JOHN. I don't want her to think too badly of me.

CONSTANCE. Of course not.

JOHN (*turning at* L.C.). But be sure it's definite.

CONSTANCE. Leave it to me.

JOHN. You're splendid, Constance. By George, no man could want a better wife.

(BENTLEY *enters up* C.)

BENTLEY. Mrs. Durham.

(MARIE-LOUISE *enters.* CONSTANCE *rises and goes up to her. They meet at* C. *and embrace warmly.* BENTLEY *exits.*)

MARIE-LOUISE. Darling, how perfectly divine to see you again. It's too, too wonderful.

CONSTANCE. My dear, how well you're looking. Are those the new pearls?

MARIE-LOUISE. Aren't they sweet? But Mortimer bought me the most heavenly emeralds when we were in India. (*Turning to* JOHN.) Oh, John, how are you?

JOHN. Oh, I'm all right, thanks.

MARIE-LOUISE (*to* CONSTANCE). I'm so glad I caught you. I should have been so disappointed to miss you. (*To* JOHN.) Where are you going?

JOHN. Nowhere. Constance is going alone.

MARIE-LOUISE. Is she? How perfectly divine. I suppose you can't get away. Are you making pots of money?

JOHN. I get along. Will you forgive me if I leave you? I've got to be off.

MARIE-LOUISE. Of course. You're always busy, aren't you? I hope we shall see something of you while Constance is away.

JOHN. Thank you very much.

MARIE-LOUISE (*moving down* R.C. *to below the sofa*). Mortimer's golf has improved. He'd love to play with you. (*She sits.*)

JOHN (*moving up* C.). Oh yes, I should love it.

(*He exits up* C. CONSTANCE *moves above the sofa to* R., *and down.*)

MARIE-LOUISE. I did so hope to find you alone. Constance, I've got heaps and heaps to tell you. Isn't it tactful of John to leave us? First of all I want to tell you how splendidly everything has turned out. You know you were quite right. I'm so glad I took your advice and made Mortimer take me away for a year.

CONSTANCE (*sitting at the* R. *end of the sofa*). Mortimer is no fool.

MARIE-LOUISE. Oh no, for a man he's really quite clever. I gave him hell, you know, for ever having suspected me, and at last he was just eating out of my hand.

CONSTANCE. I'm very glad.

MARIE-LOUISE. I owe it all to you, Constance. I made Mortimer buy you a perfectly divine star sapphire in Ceylon. I told him he owed you some sort of reparation. It cost a hundred and twenty pounds, darling, and we're taking it to Cartier's to have it set.

CONSTANCE. How thrilling.

MARIE-LOUISE. You mustn't think I'm ungrateful. Now listen, Constance, I want to tell you at once that you needn't distress yourself about me and John.

CONSTANCE. I never did.

MARIE-LOUISE (*rising and moving* L.). I know I behaved like a little beast, but I never thought you'd find out. If I had, well, you know me well enough to be positive that nothing would have induced me to have anything to do with him.

CONSTANCE. That's very nice of you!

MARIE-LOUISE (*turning, and moving in, to* L.C.). I want you to do something for me, Constance. Will you?

CONSTANCE. I'm always eager to oblige a friend.

MAIRE-LOUISE (*easing a little up* R.C.). Well, you know what John is. Of course he's a dear and all that kind of thing, but the thing's over and it's best that he should realise it at once.

CONSTANCE (*sitting erect*). Over ?

MARIE-LOUISE (*moving down, above the* L. *end of the sofa*). Of course I know he's head over heels in love with me still. I saw that the moment I came into the room. One can't blame him for that can one ?

CONSTANCE. Men do find you fascinating.

MARIE-LOUISE. But one has to think of oneself sometimes in this world. He must see that it could never be the same after we discovered that you knew all about it.

CONSTANCE. I kept it from you as long as I could.

MARIE-LOUISE. You know, I wouldn't hurt John's feelings for the world, but it's no good beating around the bush and I'm quite determined to have the thing finished and done with before you go.

CONSTANCE (*rising and breaking* R. *to the fireplace*). This is very sudden. I'm afraid it'll be an awful shock to John.

MARIE-LOUISE. I've quite made up my mind.

CONSTANCE (*thoughtfully, facing front*). There isn't much time for a very long and moving scene, but I'll see if John is in still. (*Turning to* MARIE-LOUISE.) Could you manage it in ten minutes ?

MARIE-LOUISE. Oh, but *I* can't see him. I want you to tell him.

CONSTANCE. Me !

MARIE-LOUISE (*moving down* L. *of the sofa*). You know him so well, you know just the sort of things to say to him. It's not very nice telling a man who adores you that you don't care for him in that way any more. It's so much easier for a third party.

CONSTANCE. Do you really think so ?

MARIE-LOUISE. I'm positive of it.

CONSTANCE (*easing in to below the sofa*). But if he insists on seeing you ?

MARIE-LOUISE (*going to* CONSTANCE). It's no good, Constance, I can't see him. I shall only cry and get my eyes all bunged up. You will do it for me, darling ? Please ! (*She embraces* CONSTANCE.)

CONSTANCE. I will. (*She releases herself and crosses* MARIE-LOUISE *to* C.) Now tell me the real reason why you're so determined to get rid of John without a moment's delay ?

(MARIE-LOUISE *gives a little roguish smile.*)

MARIE-LOUISE. Swear you won't tell.

CONSTANCE (*turning*). On my honour.

MARIE-LOUISE. Well, my dear, we met a perfectly divine young man on the boat. He's an A.D.C. to some Governor. He simply adores me.

CONSTANCE. And of course you adore him.

MARIE-LOUISE (*easing a little up* C.). My dear, I'm absolutely mad about him. I don't know what's going to happen.

CONSTANCE. I think we can both give a pretty shrewd guess. (*She breaks down* L. *by the low table.*)

MARIE-LOUISE. It's simply awful to have a temperament like mine. Of course you can't understand, you're cold.

CONSTANCE (*very calmly, turning*). You're an immoral little beast, Marie-Louise.

MARIE-LOUISE (*surprised and really hurt*). Constance, how can you say such a thing to me ? I think it's terribly unkind of you. I thought you liked me.

CONSTANCE. I do. I think you a liar, a humbug and a parasite, but I like you.

MARIE-LOUISE. You can't if you think such dreadful things about me.

CONSTANCE. I do. (*Moving up* L.C.) You're good-tempered and generous and sometimes amusing. I even have a certain affection for you.

MARIE-LOUISE (*smiling*). I don't believe you mean a word you say. You know how devoted I am to you.

CONSTANCE. I take people as they are and I daresay that in another twenty years you'll be the pink of propriety.

MARIE-LOUISE. Darling, I knew you didn't mean it, but you will have your little joke.

CONSTANCE (*taking* MARIE-LOUISE *up* C. *to the doors*). Now run along, darling, and I'll break the news to John. (*She opens the door.*)

MARIE-LOUISE. Well good-bye, and be gentle with him. There is no reason why we shouldn't spare him as much as possible. (*She turns at the door.*) Of course I've often wondered why with your looks you don't have more success than you do. I know now.

CONSTANCE. Tell me.

MARIE-LOUISE. You see—you're a humourist and that always puts men off.

(*She exits.* CONSTANCE *moves above the sofa, and stands, thoughtfully. A door slams off. In a moment the doors are cautiously opened and* JOHN *puts his head in.*)

JOHN. Has she gone ?

CONSTANCE. Come in. A fine night and all's well.

JOHN (*entering*). I heard the door bang. (*He closes the doors.*) You broke it to her ?

CONSTANCE. I broke it. (*She eases* R. *above the sofa.*)

JOHN (*moving down* C.). Was she awfully upset ?

CONSTANCE. Of course it was a shock, but she kept a stiff upper lip.

JOHN. Did she cry ?

CONSTANCE (*moving down* R., *to the fireplace*). No. Not exactly. To tell you the truth I think she was stunned by the blow. But of course when she gets home and realises the full extent of her loss, she'll cry like anything.

JOHN (*uncomfortably*). I hate to see a woman cry.

CONSTANCE (*easing to below the sofa*). It is painful, isn't it ? But of course it's a relief to the nerves.

JOHN (*moving to above the* L. *end of the sofa*). I think you're rather cool about it, Constance. I am not feeling any too comfortable. I shouldn't like her to think I'd treated her badly.

CONSTANCE (*moving slowly across to* L.C.). I think she quite understands that you're doing it for my sake. She knows that you have still a very great regard for her.

JOHN. But you made it quite definite, didn't you ?

CONSTANCE (*turning*). Oh, quite.

JOHN (*easing to below the* R. *end of the sofa*). I'm really very much obliged to you, Constance. (*He sits.*)

CONSTANCE. Not at all.

JOHN (*sitting back, comfortably*). At all events I'm glad to think that you'll be able to set out on your holiday with a perfectly easy mind. (*Sitting erect.*) By the way, do you want any money ? I'll write you a cheque at once.

CONSTANCE (*easing to the* L. *end of the sofa*). Oh, no, thank you. I've got plenty. I've earned fourteen hundred pounds during this year that I've been working.

JOHN. Have you, by Jove ! That's a very considerable sum.

CONSTANCE (*to below the sofa*). I'm taking two hundred of it for my holiday. (*Sitting* L. *of* JOHN.) I've spent two hundred on my clothes and on odds and ends, and the remaining thousand I've paid into your account this morning for my board and lodging during the last twelve months.

JOHN. Nonsense darling. I won't hear of such a thing. I don't want you to pay for your board and lodging.

CONSTANCE (*sitting to face* JOHN). I insist.

JOHN. Don't you love me any more ?

CONSTANCE. What has that to do with it ? Oh, you think a woman can only love a man if he keeps her. Isn't that rating your powers of fascination too modestly ? What about your charm and good-humour ?

JOHN. Don't be absurd, Constance. I can perfectly well afford to support you in your proper station. To offer me a thousand pounds for your board and lodging is almost insulting.

CONSTANCE. Don't you think it's the kind of insult you could bring yourself to swallow ? One can do a lot of amusing things with a thousand pounds.

JOHN (*rising*). I wouldn't dream of taking it. (*Crossing* L. *towards the desk.*) I never liked the idea of your going into business. I thought you had quite enough to do looking after the house and so forth.

CONSTANCE (*without turning*). Have you been less comfortable since I began working ?

JOHN (*turning at* L.). No, I can't say I have. (*Moving to the* L. *end of the sofa.*) Anyhow you wanted to work and I yielded. I thought in point of fact it would be a very pleasant occupation for you, but heaven knows, I wasn't expecting to profit financially by it.

CONSTANCE (*still turned slightly away*). No, I'm sure you weren't.

JOHN. Constance, I could never help thinking that your determination had something to do with Marie-Louise.

(*There is a moment's pause and when* CONSTANCE *speaks it is not without seriousness.*)

CONSTANCE (*without moving*). Haven't you wondered why I never reproached you for your affair with Marie-Louise ?

JOHN. Yes. I could only ascribe it to your unfathomable goodness.

CONSTANCE (*by the fireplace*). You were wrong. I felt I hadn't the right to reproach you. (*She is slightly turned away.*)

JOHN. What do you mean ? You had every right.

CONSTANCE. No. You no longer desired me.

(JOHN *turns and moves below the piano stool.*)

(*Turning to look across at him.*) And if you didn't desire me, what use was I to you ? You've seen how small a share I take in providing you with the comfort of a well-ordered home.

JOHN. You were the mother of my child. (*He sits on the piano stool.*)

CONSTANCE (*moving below the sofa to the* L. *end of it*). Let us not exaggerate the importance of that, John. (*She sits on the* L. *arm of the sofa.*) I owe you a debt of gratitude for never letting me see that I was no more than a costly and at times inconvenient ornament.

JOHN (*rising; a little indignant*). I never looked on you as an inconvenient ornament. (*More gently, moving a little towards her.*) Don't you think a man may have gratitude to a woman for the love he has had for her in the past ?

CONSTANCE (*with a little smile*). I think gratitude is often very strong in men so long as it demands no particular sacrifices !

JOHN (*breaking a little down* L.). Well, it's a curious way of looking at things—but obviously I've reason to be thankful for it. (*Turning.*) But you knew what was going on long before it came out. What happened then that made you make up your mind to go into business ?

(CONSTANCE *rises and moves to* C.)

CONSTANCE. I thought I should very much like to be in a position where, if I felt inclined to, I could tell you, with calm and courtesy, but with determination—to go to hell.

(*A slight pause.*)

JOHN. And are you in that position now ?

CONSTANCE. Precisely. (*Smiles at his bewilderment.*) My dear, there is only one freedom that is really important, and that is economic freedom. Well, I have it . . . (*moving away* R. *to below the sofa*) and upon my soul, it's the most enjoyable sensation I can remember since I ate my first strawberry ice. (*She sits.*)

JOHN (*moving a little up* C.). You know, I would sooner you had made me scenes for a month on end like any ordinary woman, and nagged my life out, than that you should harbour this cold rancour against me.

CONSTANCE. My poor darling, what are you talking about? I harbour no rancour. Why, I'm devoted to you.

JOHN (*moving* R.C., *above and* L. *of the sofa*). Do you mean to tell me that you've done all this without any intention of making me feel a perfect cad?

CONSTANCE. On my honour. (*Looking up at him.*) Don't you believe me?

JOHN. Yes—oddly enough, I do. (*Easing* R., *above the sofa.*) You are a remarkable woman, Constance.

CONSTANCE. I know, but keep it to yourself. You don't want to give a dog a bad name.

JOHN (*above the sofa*, R. *of* CONSTANCE—*with an affectionate smile*). I wish I could get away. I don't half like the idea of your travelling by yourself.

CONSTANCE. Oh, but I'm not. Didn't I tell you?

JOHN. No.

CONSTANCE. I meant to. I'm going with Bernard.

JOHN. Oh. You never said so. Who else?

CONSTANCE. Nobody.

JOHN. Oh! (*He is rather taken aback at the news.*) Isn't that rather odd?

CONSTANCE. No. Why?

JOHN (*not knowing at all how to take it; easing down* R. *of the sofa*). Well, it's not usual for a young woman to take six weeks' holiday with a man who can hardly be described as old enough to be her father.

CONSTANCE. Bernard's just about the same age as you.

JOHN (*moving to the fireplace*). Don't you think it'll make people gossip a bit?

CONSTANCE. I haven't gone out of my way to spread the news. In fact, now I come to think of it, I haven't told anyone but you, and you, I am sure, will be discreet.

(JOHN *suddenly feels that his collar is a little too tight for him and with his fingers he tries to loosen it.*)

JOHN. You're pretty certain to be seen by someone who knows you, and they're bound to talk.

CONSTANCE. Oh, I don't think so. You see we're motoring all the way and we neither of us care for frequented places.

JOHN (*uncomfortably; moving across to* C., *below the sofa*). Of course I am not so silly as to think that because a man and a woman go away together it is necessary to believe the worst about them, but (*turning*) you can't deny that it is rather unconventional. I wouldn't for a moment suggest that there'll be anything between you, but it's inevitable that ordinary persons should think there was.

CONSTANCE (*as cool as a cucumber*).   I've always thought that ordinary persons had more sense than the clever ones are ready to credit them with.

JOHN (*deliberately*).   What on earth do you mean ?

CONSTANCE.   Why, of course we're going as man and wife, John.

JOHN (*moving sharply to the* L. *end of the sofa*).   Don't be a fool, Constance.   You don't know what you're talking about.   That's not funny at all.

CONSTANCE.   But, my poor John, whom do you take us for ? Am I so unattractive that what I'm telling you is incredible ? Why else would I go with Bernard? If I merely wanted a companion I'd go with a woman.

JOHN.   I may be very stupid, but I don't seem to be able to understand what you're saying.   Do you really mean me to believe that Bernard Kersal is your lover ?

CONSTANCE.   Certainly not.

JOHN.   Then what *are* you talking about ?

CONSTANCE.   My dear, I can't put it any plainer.   I'm going away for six weeks' holiday and Bernard has very kindly offered to come with me.

JOHN.   And where do I come in ?

CONSTANCE.   You don't come in.

(JOHN *breaks down* L.)

You stay at home and look after your patients.

JOHN (*turning and moving up to* C.; *trying his best to control himself*).   I flatter myself I'm a sensible man.   I'm not going to fly into a passion.   Many men would stamp and rave or break the furniture.   I have no intention of being melodramatic, but you must allow me to say that what you've just told me is very surprising.

CONSTANCE.   Just for a moment, perhaps, but I'm sure you have only to familiarise yourself with the notion in order to become reconciled to it.

JOHN (*crossing down* R. *to the fireplace*).   I'm doubtful whether I shall have time to do that, for I feel uncommonly as though I were about to have an apoplectic stroke.

CONSTANCE.   Undo your collar then.

JOHN (*turning*).   What makes you think that I am going to allow you to go ?

CONSTANCE (*good-humouredly*).   Chiefly the fact that you can't prevent me.

JOHN.   I can't bring myself to believe that you mean what you say.   I don't know whatever put such an idea into your head.

CONSTANCE (*casually*).   I thought a change might do me good.

JOHN.   Nonsense.   Do you expect me to sit still and let this man take my wife away from under my very nose ? (*Crossing above the sofa to* C.) I wonder you don't ask me to shake hands with him and wish him good luck. (*He stands by the* R. *side of the piano.*)

CONSTANCE. That's just what I am going to do. He's coming here in a few minutes to say good-bye to you.

JOHN (*moving down* L.C.). I shall knock him down. (*He turns up to the piano stool.*)

CONSTANCE. I wouldn't take any risks in your place. I'm under the impression that he's very nippy with his left.

JOHN (*moving down to* R. *of the low table,* L.). I shall have great pleasure in telling him exactly what I think of him.

CONSTANCE. Why? (*Rising.*) Have you forgotten that I am charming to Marie-Louise? (*Moving to* C.) We were the best of friends. She never bought a hat without asking me to go and help her choose it.

JOHN (*turning*). Is he in love with you?

CONSTANCE. Madly. Didn't you know?

JOHN. I? How should I?

CONSTANCE. He's been here a great deal during the last year. Were you under the impression that he only came to see you?

JOHN. I never paid any attention to him. I thought him rather dull. (*He breaks* L. *to the desk.*)

CONSTANCE. He is rather dull. But he's very sweet.

JOHN (*turning and moving in a little*). What sort of a man is it who eats a fellow's food and drinks his wine and then makes love to his wife behind his back.

CONSTANCE (*moving to above the sofa*). A man very like you, John, I should say.

(JOHN *turns away impatiently.* BENTLEY *enters, up* C.)

BENTLEY. Mrs. Culver.

(MRS. CULVER *enters.* BENTLEY *exits.*)

CONSTANCE (*moving to* C.). Oh, mother, how sweet of you to come. I was so hoping I'd see you before I left. (*She glances at* JOHN *and then turns again to* MRS. CULVER.) John's in a temper.

MRS. CULVER. Nonsense, John's never in a temper.

JOHN (*down* L., *below the piano*). That's what you think, Mrs. Culver. Yes, I am in a temper. I'm in a filthy temper. Are you a party to this plan of Constance's?

CONSTANCE (*moving* R., *above the sofa*). No, mother doesn't know.

JOHN. Can't you do something to stop it? You have some influence over her. You must see that the thing's preposterous.

MRS. CULVER (*moving away* R., *to below the* L. *end of the sofa*). My dear boy, I haven't the ghost of an idea what you're talking about.

JOHN. She's going to Italy with Bernard Kersal. Alone.

MRS. CULVER (*turning; with a stare*). It's not true. How d'you know?

JOHN (*moving to* C.). She's just told me so, as bold as brass, out of a blue sky. She mentioned it in the course of conversation as if she were saying, " Darling, your coat wants brushing."

Mrs. Culver (*turning to look at* Constance).   Is it true,
Constance ?

Constance (*easing down, R. of the sofa*).   Quite.

(Mrs. Culver *sits at the L. end of the sofa.*)

Mrs. Culver.   But haven't you been getting on with John ?
I always thought you two were as happy as the day is long.

John.   So did I.   We've never had the shadow of a quarrel.
We've always got on.

Mrs. Culver.   Don't you love John any more, darling ?

Constance (*sitting on the R. arm of the sofa*).   Yes, I'm devoted
to him.

John.   How can you be devoted to a man when you're going to
do him the greatest injury that a woman can do to a man ?

Constance (*calmly and pleasantly*).   Don't be idiotic, John.   I'm
going to do you no more injury than you did me a year ago.

John (*thinking quite erroneously that he sees light*).   Are you doing
this in order to pay me out for Marie-Louise ?

Constance (*as before*).   Don't be such a fool, John.   Nothing is
further from my thoughts.

Mrs. Culver.   The circumstances are entirely different.   It was
very naughty of John to deceive you, but he's sorry for what he
did, and he's been punished for it.

(John *moves away down L. and sits.*)

We all know that unchastity has no moral effect on men.   They
can be perfectly promiscuous and remain upright, industrious, and
reliable.   It's quite different with women.   It ruins their character.

Constance.   That's because they were giving away something
that wasn't theirs to give.   But I'm not dependent on John.   I'm
economically independent, and therefore I claim my sexual
independence.   I have this afternoon paid into John's account
one thousand pounds for my year's keep.

John (*jumping up*).   I refuse to take it.

Constance.   Well, you'll damned well have to.

Mrs. Culver.   There's no object in losing your tempers.

Constance.   I have mine under perfect control.

(John *sits again.*)

Mrs. Culver.   Are you in love with Bernard ?

Constance.   To tell you the truth, I haven't quite made up my
mind.   How does one know if one's in love ?

Mrs. Culver.   My dear, I only know of one test.   Could you
use his toothbrush ?

Constance.   No.   (*She rises and breaks R. to the fireplace.*)

Mrs. Culver.   Then you're not in love with him.

Constance.   There's something in his devotion which gives
me a funny little feeling in my heart.   (*Moving above the R. end of
the sofa.   To* Mrs. Culver.)   I should like to do something to show

him that I'm not ungrateful. (*She moves towards* C. *as she continues.*) You see, in six weeks he goes back to China—for seven years. (*Turning.*) I'm thirty-six now, and he adores me ; in seven years I shall be forty-three. A woman of forty-three is often charming, but it's seldom that a man of fifty-five is crazy about her. I came to the conclusion that it was now or never, and so . . .

(BENTLEY *enters up* C.)

BENTLEY. Mr. Bernard Kersal is here, madam.
CONSTANCE (*below and* L. *of* BENTLEY). Show him up, Bentley.
BENTLEY. Very good, madam.

(*He exits.* MRS. CULVER *rises, eases* R., *and turns.*)

JOHN (*rising*). Do you expect me to receive him as if I were blissfully unconscious of your plans ?
CONSTANCE. It would be more comfortable.
MRS. CULVER (*moving to* L. *of the sofa*). Constance, is there nothing I can say to make you reconsider your decision ?
CONSTANCE. Nothing, darling.
MRS. CULVER (*moving to* C.). Then I may as well save my breath. I'll slip away before he comes.
CONSTANCE. Oh, all right. (*They kiss.*) Good-bye mother. I'll send you a lot of picture postcards.
MRS. CULVER. I don't approve of you, Constance, and I can't pretend that I do.

(*She turns up to the door as* BENTLEY *enters followed by* BERNARD.)

BENTLEY. Mr. Kersal.
MRS. CULVER. How do you do, Bernard, and good-bye. I'm just going.
BERNARD. Oh, I'm so sorry. Good-bye.

(MRS. CULVER *exits.* BENTLEY *is about to follow.*)

CONSTANCE. Oh, Bentley.
BENTLEY (*checking*). Yes, madam ?
CONSTANCE. Get my things down and put them in a taxi, will you ?
BENTLEY. Very good, madam.
BERNARD. Are you just starting ? It's lucky I came when I did. I should have hated to miss you. (*He exchanges nods and smiles with* JOHN.)
CONSTANCE (*to* BENTLEY). And let me know when the taxi's here.
BENTLEY. Yes, madam.

(*He exits.*)

CONSTANCE (*to* BERNARD, *smiling*). Now I can attend to you. (*She crosses down* R.C., *below the* L. *arm of the sofa.*)
BERNARD. Are you looking forward to your holiday ?
CONSTANCE. Immensely. (*She sits on the* L. *arm of the sofa.*)

I've never gone on a jaunt like this before, and I'm really excited.

BERNARD (*easing to* R.C.). You're going alone, aren't you ?

CONSTANCE. Oh yes, quite alone.

BERNARD (*turning and moving* C., *addressing* JOHN). It's rotten for you not to be able to get away, old man.

JOHN (*at* L.C.). Rotten.

BERNARD. I suppose these are the penalties of greatness. I can quite understand that you have to think of your patients first.

JOHN. Quite. (*He moves* L. *to the desk.*)

CONSTANCE. Of course John doesn't very much care for Italy.

BERNARD (*turning to* CONSTANCE). Oh, are you going to Italy ? I thought you said Spain.

JOHN (*at* L., *over his shoulder*). No, she always said Italy.

BERNARD (*to* JOHN). Oh, well, that's hardly your mark, is it, old boy ? Though I believe there are some sporting links on the Lake of Como.

JOHN (*looking out of the window*). Are there ? (*He pretends to attend to something at the desk.*)

BERNARD (*to* CONSTANCE). I suppose there's no chance of your being anywhere near Genoa towards the end of July ?

CONSTANCE. I don't really know. My plans are quite vague.

BERNARD. I was only asking because I'm sailing from Genoa. It would be fun if we met there.

JOHN (*over his shoulder*). Great fun.

CONSTANCE. I hope you'll see a lot of John while I'm away. I'm afraid he'll be a trifle lonely, poor darling. Why don't you dine together one day next week ?

BERNARD (*moving a little towards* CONSTANCE). I'm terribly sorry, but you know I'm going away.

(JOHN *moves* L.C., *listening.*)

CONSTANCE. Oh are you ? I thought you were going to stay in London till you had to start for China.

BERNARD. I meant to, but my doctor has ordered me to go away for a cure.

JOHN   What sort of a cure ?

BERNARD (*at* C.). Oh, just a cure. He says I want bucking up.

JOHN. Oh, does he ? (*Moving a pace nearer* BERNARD.) What's the name of your doctor ?

BERNARD   No one you ever heard of. A man I knew in the war.

JOHN. Oh !

BERNARD. So I'm afraid this is good-bye. (*With a pace towards* JOHN.) Of course it's a wrench leaving London, especially as I don't expect to be in Europe again for some years, but I always think it rather silly not to take a man's advice when you've asked for it.

JOHN. More especially when he's charged you several guineas.

(BERNARD *turns to* CONSTANCE.)

CONSTANCE. I'm sorry. I was counting on you to keep John out of mischief during my absence.

BERNARD (*moving towards* CONSTANCE). I'm not sure if I could guarantee to do that. But we might have done a few theatres together and had a game or two of golf.

CONSTANCE. It would have been jolly, wouldn't it, John ?

JOHN. Very jolly. (*He goes to the low table* L. *for a cigarette.*)

(BENTLEY *enters.*)

BENTLEY. The taxi's waiting, madam.

CONSTANCE. Thank you.

(BENTLEY *exits.*)

BERNARD. I'll take myself off.

(CONSTANCE *rises.*)

CONSTANCE. We shall miss you terribly. It's been a great comfort to John to think that there was someone to take me out when he had to be away on one of his operations. (*Looking at* JOHN.) Hasn't it darling ?

JOHN. Yes, darling.

CONSTANCE. When he knew I was with you he never worried. Did you, darling ?

JOHN. No, darling.

BERNARD. I'm awfully glad if I've been able to make myself useful. Don't forget me entirely, will you ?

CONSTANCE (*to* BERNARD). We're not likely to do that (*to* JOHN) are we, darling ?

JOHN. No, darling.

BERNARD. And if you ever have a moment to spare you will write to me, won't you ? (*To* JOHN.) You don't know how much it means to us exiles.

CONSTANCE (*to* BERNARD). Of course we will. We'll both write. (*To* JOHN.) Won't we, darling ?

JOHN. Yes, darling.

CONSTANCE. John writes such a good letter. So chatty, you know, and amusing.

BERNARD. That's a promise. (*Crossing to* JOHN.) Well, good-bye, old boy. Have a good time.

JOHN. Thanks, old man.

(*They shake hands.* BERNARD *crosses to* CONSTANCE.)

BERNARD. Good-bye, Constance. There's so much I want to say to you that I don't know where to begin.

JOHN. I don't want to hurry you, but the taxi is just ticking its head off.

BERNARD. John is so matter-of-fact. Well, I'll say nothing then but God bless you.

CONSTANCE. Au revoir.

(*They shake hands.*)

BERNARD. Good-bye. (*Moving up* C.) If you do go to Genoa, you will let me know, won't you ? (*Turning at the door.*) If you send a line to my club it'll be forwarded at once.
CONSTANCE. Oh, all right.
BERNARD. Good-bye.

(*He gives them both a friendly nod and exits.* CONSTANCE *begins to giggle, sits on the sofa and is seized with uncontrollable laughter.*)

JOHN (*moving to above and* L. *of the sofa*). Will you kindly tell me what there is to laugh at ? If you think it amuses me to stand here like patience on a monument and have my leg pulled you're mistaken. What did you mean by all that balderdash about meeting you by chance in Genoa ?
CONSTANCE (*still laughing*). He was throwing you off the scent.
JOHN. The man's a drivelling idiot. (*He breaks down* L. *and puts out his cigarette.*)
CONSTANCE. D'you think so ? (*Gradually recovering.*) I thought he was rather ingenious. Considering he hasn't had very much practice in this sort of thing I thought he did very well.
JOHN (*moving up to* R. *of the piano stool*). Of course if you're determined to find him a pattern of perfection it's useless for me to attempt to argue. (*Moving to* C.) But honestly, speaking without prejudice for or against, I'm sorry to think of you throwing yourself away on a man like that.
CONSTANCE. Perhaps it's natural that a man and his wife should differ in their estimate of her prospective lover.
JOHN (*moving to* L. *of the sofa*). You're not going to tell me he's better-looking than I am.
CONSTANCE. No. You have always been my ideal of manly beauty.
JOHN. I don't think you can honestly say he's more amusing than I am.
CONSTANCE. No, I honestly can't.
JOHN (*angrily; crossing down* R. *to the fireplace*). Then in Heaven's name why do you want to go away with him ?
CONSTANCE. Shall I tell you ? For ten years I've been very happy in your affections, John. We've been the best and dearest friends, but now just for a little while I hanker for something else. Do you grudge it me ? I want to be loved.
JOHN (*turning*). But, my dear, I'll love you. (*Moving to the sofa and sitting on her* R.) I've been a brute, I've neglected you, it's not too late and you're the only woman I've ever really cared for. I'll chuck everything and we'll go away together.
CONSTANCE. The prospect doesn't thrill me.
JOHN. Come, darling, have a heart. I gave up Marie-Louise. Surely you can give up Bernard.

CONSTANCE. But you gave up Marie-Louise to please yourself, not to please me.

JOHN. Don't be a little beast, Constance. Come away with me. we'll have such a wonderful time.

CONSTANCE. Oh, my poor John, I didn't work so hard to gain my economic independence in order to go on a honeymoon with my own husband.

JOHN. Do you think I can't be a lover as well as a husband ?

CONSTANCE. My dear, no one can make yesterday's cold mutton into tomorrow's lamb cutlets.

JOHN (*rising*). You know what you're doing. (*Moving below the sofa to* L.C.) I was determined in future to be a model husband and you're driving me right into the arms of Marie-Louise. (*Turning at* L.C.) I give you my word of honour that the moment you leave this house I shall drive straight to her door. (*He moves* L. *to the desk.*)

CONSTANCE. I should hate you to have a fruitless journey. (*Rising.*) I'm afraid you won't find her at home. She has a new young man and she says he's too divine.

(JOHN *turns and moves in to* L.C.)

JOHN. What !

CONSTANCE. He's the A.D.C. to a Colonial Governor. (*Moving round the* L. *end of the sofa.*) She came here today to ask me to break the news to you that henceforth everything was over between you.

JOHN (*up* L.C., *below the piano stool*). I hope you told her first that I was firmly resolved to terminate a connection that could only cause you pain.

CONSTANCE (*above the* L. *end of the sofa*). I couldn't. She was in such a fearful hurry to give me her message.

JOHN (*easing to* C.). Really, Constance, for your own pride I should have thought you wouldn't like her to make a perfect fool of me. Any other woman would have said : " What a strange coincidence. Why it's only half an hour since John told me he had made up his mind never to see you again." (*Breaking down* L.) But of course you don't care two straws for me any more, that's quite evident. (*He turns away from her and takes another cigarette, lighting it savagely.*)

CONSTANCE (*easing to* R.C.). Oh, don't be unjust, darling. I shall always care for you. I may be unfaithful, but I am constant. I always think that's my most endearing quality.

(*Enter* BENTLEY *up* C.)

JOHN (*turning; irritably*). What is it ?

BENTLEY. I thought madam had forgotten that the taxi was at the door.

JOHN. Go to hell.

BENTLEY.   Very good, sir.

(*He exits.*)

CONSTANCE.   I don't see why you should be rude to him. Bernard will pay the taxi. (*Moving up* C., *to* R. *of the piano.*) Anyhow I must go now or he'll begin to think I'm not coming. (*Turning.*) Good-bye, darling. I hope you'll get on all right in my absence. Just give the cook her head and you'll have no trouble. (*A slight pause.*) Won't you say good-bye to me ?

JOHN (*crossing* R., *below the sofa*).   Go to the devil.

CONSTANCE.   All right. I shall be back in six weeks.

JOHN (*turning, below the* R. *end of the sofa*).   Back ? Where ?

CONSTANCE.   Here.

JOHN.   Here ? *Here* ? (*Taking a pace to the* L. *end of the sofa.*) Do you think I'm going to take you back ?

CONSTANCE (*easing a little down,* C.).   I don't see why not. When you've had time to reflect, you'll realise that you have no reason to blame me. After all, I'm taking from you nothing that you want.

JOHN.   Are you aware that I can divorce you for this ?

CONSTANCE.   Quite. But I married very prudently. I took the precaution to marry a gentleman and I know that you could never bring yourself to divorce me for doing no more than you did yourself.

JOHN (*breaking away* R.).   I wouldn't divorce you. (*Turning up* R. *of the sofa and facing her.*) I wouldn't expose my worst enemy to the risk of marrying a woman who's capable of treating her husband as you're treating me.

CONSTANCE (*easing a little up* C., *but still looking at him*).   Well, then, shall I come back ?

(*A slight pause.*)

JOHN (*moving along the back of the sofa to* L. *of it*).   You are the most maddening, wilful, capricious, wrong-headed, delightful and enchanting woman man was ever cursed with having for a wife. Yes, damn you, come back.

(CONSTANCE *lightly kisses her hand to him and slips out, slamming the door behind her.*)

CURTAIN.

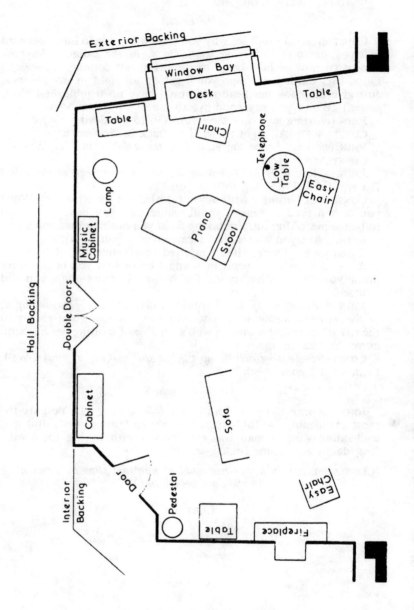

FURNITURE AND PROPERTY PLOT

Carpet on stage. Strip carpets outside all doors.

Long curtains at the window. Rug at the fireplace.

(*The curtains for Act III should be of a different colour and pattern from those used in the previous acts.*)

On the walls: Some very good water colours and etchings.

Sofa, with cushions (R.C.).

Easy chair (*down* R.).

Easy chair (*down* L.).

Round low table (*above chair down* L.). *On it:* A box of cigarettes. An ashtray. Dial telephone. A novel.

Standard lamp (*up* L.).

Baby grand piano. *On it:* Usual dressings, and one or two pieces of music.

Long piano stool.

(NOTE.—*If a piano is not available, a small settee should be placed where the piano stool would be, with a round table behind it, on which a bowl of flowers, one or two photographs in silver frames, or other dressings, as desired.*)

Writing desk. (L. *in the window bay.*) *On it:* Blotter, diary, inkstand, stationery cabinet, calendar, etc.

Chair (*at the desk*).

Small table (R. *above the fireplace*). *On it:* A table lamp.

Pedestal with tall vase (*above the small table*, R.).

On the mantelpiece:—A clock. Two framed photographs, or a few pieces of porcelain, or other ornaments. Electric wall brackets above the mantel.

Glass-fronted cabinet (R. *of the* C. *doors*). *In it:* Some fine pieces of porcelain and other objets d'art.

Music cabinet (L. *of the doors* C.).

Side table (*above the window bay*, L.). *On it:* A tall vase for flowers, and other dressings.

Small occasional table, or nest of tables (*down* L., *below the window bay*).

Bell push (*in the back wall*, L. *of the doors*).

Illustrated periodicals on stage for opening of Acts I and II.

PERSONAL PROPERTIES

ACT I.

CONSTANCE.	Handbag, containing three handkerchiefs. Three or four small packages or parcels in London shop wrappings.
BERNARD.	Lighter, or silver match box.
MARTHA.	Handbag.
MRS. CULVER.	Handbag.
BARBARA.	Handbag.

(*Note.—All ladies' handbags must be different in each Act.*)

ACT II.

BENTLEY.	Visiting card on a silver salver.
MORTIMER.	A gold cigarette case. (JOHN'S.)

ACT III.

On the desk:	Letter for CONSTANCE. An envelope. Some postage stamps. A box of chocolates.

LIGHTING

The lighting tor all the Acts may be the same and should consist of mingled No. 36 (Lavender) and No. 51 (Gold) full in the battens, and at half in the floats. In Act I the lighting may be a little deeper. Similar lighting on the interior backings.

The exterior backing is flooded white frost in Acts I and III. In Act II this may be deepened with No. 3 (straw).

There are no lighting changes during the action.

MADE AND PRINTED IN GREAT BRITAIN BY
BUTLER & TANNER LTD, FROME AND LONDON
MADE IN ENGLAND